# THE HOPE OF GLORY

# THE
# HOPE
# OF
# GLORY

*Reflections on
the Last Words of Jesus
from the Cross*

## JON MEACHAM

CONVERGENT
NEW YORK

Illustration credits appear on page 127.

Hardback ISBN 9780593236666
eBook ISBN 9780593236673

Printed in the United States of America on acid-free paper

convergentbooks.com

FIRST EDITION

2 4 6 8 9 7 5 3 1

*Book design by Carole Lowenstein*

*For now we see through a glass, darkly,*
*but then face to face.*
—The First Epistle of Paul to the Corinthians

*It is far better to accept teachings with reason and wisdom*
*than with mere faith.*
—Origen of Alexandria

# CONTENTS

# THE HOPE OF GLORY

# PROLOGUE

# In the Beginning

*But we preach Christ crucified, unto the Jews a stumbling
block, and unto the Greeks foolishness. . . . God hath chosen
the foolish things of the world to confound the wise; and
God hath chosen the weak things of the world
to confound the things which are mighty.*

—THE FIRST EPISTLE OF PAUL
TO THE CORINTHIANS

*In the world ye shall have tribulation:
but be of good cheer; I have overcome the world.*

—JESUS OF NAZARETH,
THE GOSPEL OF JOHN

IT WAS ONLY A BRIEF MOMENT, a small, seemingly throwaway remark in the midst of the most significant interview in history. In the Gospel of John, Jesus of Nazareth has been arrested and brought before Pontius Pilate, the Roman governor of Judea. "So you are a king?" Pilate asks, and Jesus says: "You say that I am a king. For this I was born, and for this I have come into the world, to bear witness to the truth. Every one who is of the truth hears my voice." Then, in what I imagine to be a cynical, world-weary tone, Pilate replies: "What is truth?"

What, indeed? Jesus says nothing in response, and Pilate's question is left hanging—an open query in the middle of John's rendering of the Passion. The search for an answer unfolds even now, for the hunger for truth—about the visible and the invisible, the seen and the unseen, the hoped-for and the feared—is among the most fundamental of appetites.

And that perennial quest for a reply to Pilate tends to take religious form. "All men need the gods," Homer wrote, and nothing since antiquity—not the Scientific Revolution, not the Enlightenment, not Darwin, not *anything*—has altered the impulse of human beings to organize stories and create systems of belief that draw on the past, give shape to the present, and promise a future of justice, mercy, and peace. "Gods," the Protestant theologian Paul Tillich wrote in the middle of the twentieth century, "are beings who transcend the realm of ordinary experience in power and meaning, with whom men have relations which surpass ordinary relations in intensity and significance."

For Christians, the central truth of existence—our ultimate concern, in a phrase of Tillich's—is captured in the death and resurrection of Jesus. Without Good Friday, there is no Easter; without Easter, there is no deliverance from evil; without deliverance from evil, there is no victory of light over dark, of love over hate, of life over death.

Yet that victory is the radical, revolutionary, and essential promise of Christianity—a promise revealed to us in the Passion of Jesus. The work of discerning—or, depending on your point of view, *assigning*—meaning to Good Friday and to the story of the empty tomb is a historical as well as a theological process, as was the construction of the faith that has shaped, and is shaping, the lives of billions of believers.

I am one among that innumerable company, and this book is a series of reflections on the Last Words of Jesus from the cross—words spoken on a Friday afternoon that is at once impossibly remote and yet imaginatively close to hand. It is a devotional work, not a scholarly one. I am an Episcopalian who was raised and educated in the faith, and I would be disheartened if my own young children were to turn away from the church in which they have grown up. I am, however, in no sense an evangelical, for I do not share the view that faith in Jesus is the only route to salvation, nor am I determined to convert others to my point of view. "It does me no injury for my neighbor to say there are twenty gods, or no god," Thomas Jefferson remarked. "It neither picks my pocket nor breaks my leg." In a sermon, John Leland—a leading Baptist preacher in Virginia and Massachusetts in the eighteenth and early nineteenth centuries—once observed, "Experience teaches us that men who are equally wise and good may differ in political as well as in theological or mathematical opinions." Some fourteen hundred years earlier, in the fourth century, the Roman writer Symmachus, arguing against Christians who wanted to remove an altar to the pagan deity Victory, said, "We cannot attain to so great a mystery by one way." I agree.

So what do I believe? I adhere to the broad outlines of the Christian faith as it has come down through the Anglican tradition. I profess the creeds, I confess my (many) sins, I make my communion, I say my prayers. And I believe that in so doing I am taking part in a drama whose ultimate purposes I cannot yet—and may never—fully grasp but in which I invest my hopes that someday, in some way, all things will be made new.

An important note: Though this book began as a series of sermons—which are, by definition, discourses on religious subjects—it is about illumination, not conversion. I am sharing these meditations in the hope that a sense of history and an appreciation of theology might help readers make more sense of the cross in a world too much given to the competing forces of hostile skepticism, blind acceptance, or remote indifference. In the Hebrew Bible, in the midst of great suffering, Job proclaims a great faith: "I know that my Redeemer liveth, and that he shall stand at the latter day upon the earth." If Job could *know,* then at least we can *hope.*

At the heart of my own hope is the belief that the God of Abraham (whom I also believe is God the Father of the Holy Trinity) is the architect of a creation that has fallen into corruption and disorder. The redemption of that creation has been set in motion by the Passion, crucifixion, and resurrection of a preacher and wonder worker in first-century Judea. In the tradition I inherited, that preacher was a great moral teacher: His Sermon on the Mount and his frequently repeated messages, rooted in the scriptures of Israel, about the centrality of love can hardly be improved upon as guides to goodness and generosity. He does not, however, endure because he offered a corner of the Roman-dominated world a message of radical love. He endures not only because of what he *said* but because of who he *was*—in the words of Peter, "the Christ, the Son of the living God." Christianity's foundational belief is that Jesus was in fact the "Christ"—in Greek, the "anointed one"—who died and rose again to redeem and restore a fallen world that is to be reborn as what

John the Divine called "a new heaven and a new earth." *That* is what Peter's confession means—and it is what Christians mean when they proclaim Jesus to be Lord and predict his coming again, even if they are not particularly clear on the details of what that entails.

Whether one believes or disbelieves or dwells, as so many of us do, somewhere in between, tacking now toward one pole and then toward another and back again (and again and again), attention must be paid. "Jesus means something to our world because a mighty spiritual force streams forth from Him and flows through our time also," Albert Schweitzer wrote in his landmark *The Quest of the Historical Jesus.* "This fact can neither be shaken nor confirmed by any historical discovery. It is the solid foundation of Christianity."

The English novelist and biographer A. N. Wilson put the matter this way: "The strange fact is that the figure of Jesus remains, even in a world where institutional Christianity would appear to be on its last legs, and where religious belief itself, in the West at least, would appear to be rapidly on the decline. Jesus is a shadowy figure historically, but he remains doggedly there, and . . . we remain aware of him, not as a mystical presence, but not as a figure of pure legend, either. He is more real than Robin Hood or King Arthur."

Jesus's mission, as defined by Paul, was seen as part of the story of Israel, a fulfillment (if an unexpected one) of the promise God had made to Abraham in Genesis. "And I will make of thee a great nation, and I will bless thee, and make thy name great; and thou shalt be a blessing," the Lord tells Abram—later renamed Abraham, or "father of many nations"—"And I will bless them that bless thee, and curse him that curseth thee: and in thee shall all families of the earth be blessed."

Hence the familiar phrase "in accordance with the scriptures," by which the New Testament authors meant in accordance with their unique first-century interpretation of the existing scriptural saga of Israel's captivity and hope for restoration. "For I delivered to you as of first importance what I also received," Paul wrote in First Corinthians, "that Christ died for our sins in accordance with the scriptures, that he was buried, that he was raised on the third day . . . and that he appeared first to Cephas, and then to the twelve." What did it all mean? "For God so loved the world," John was to write, "that he gave his only begotten Son, that whosoever believeth in him should not perish, but have everlasting life."

In the Christian worldview, the healing of God's creatures and of the creation writ large is the redemptive work of a crucified and resurrected Jesus. To put immensely complicated matters simply, the understanding that emerged in the first centuries after Jesus was that the world, in the grip of evil since the expulsion from Eden, required a sacrifice of world-shattering magnitude to rescue creation from darkness, appetite, and ambition. This *theological* framework is based on *historical* fact: Jesus was crucified and died. Then, on the third day—Sunday morning—some of his female disciples found his tomb to be empty, and his followers soon believed that the risen Jesus was moving among them. An assent to the truth of such a cosmology has been a weapon in the struggle to navigate a tragic and taxing world of injustice, pain, and death. "The shield of faith," the Epistle to the Ephesians proclaims, "can quench all the flaming darts of the evil one."

Why the Lord God of Hosts would need to do anything to redeem his own creation is as mysterious to us as the reason why He would create a world in the first place and, having created it, why he would populate it with human beings whose free will would lead to sin and suffering. God, the distinguished rabbi Abraham Joshua Heschel said in 1967, "did not make it easy for us to have faith in Him, to remain faithful to Him. *This is our tragedy:* the insecurity of faith, the unbearable burden of our commitment. The facts that deny the divine are mighty indeed; the arguments of agnosticism are eloquent, the events that defy Him are spectacular. . . . Our faith is fragile, never immune to error, distortion, or deception. There are no final proofs for the existence of God, Father and Creator of all. There are only witnesses. Supreme among them are the prophets of Israel." And, for our purposes, the authors of the New Testament.

We are all, in a sense, like the Greek philosophers who came to Paul in Athens seeking clarity about the Christian message. "May we know what this new teaching is that you are presenting?" they asked him at the Areopagus. "It sounds rather strange to us, so we would like to know what it means." The apostle then preached the gospel, saying that God, through Jesus, " 'will have the world judged in righteousness by a man whom he has appointed, and of this he has given assurance to all by raising him from the dead.' When they heard of the resurrection of the dead, some scoffed; but others said, 'We will hear you again about this.' " Some scoff still; others endeavor to hear it still.

To me, to be reflexively dismissive of faith is as self-defeating as being reflexively dismissive of the role of the mind in the life of the world and of the great religions. That we cannot know everything does not mean we can know nothing. With Paul, the faithful must recognize that, for now, we can only squint to "see through a glass, darkly." With Shakespeare, the secular should remember that, as Hamlet remarked to Horatio, "There are more things in heaven and earth . . . than are dreamt of in your philosophy." Humility is in many ways the beginning of wisdom. "Reason's last step is the recognition that there are an infinite number of things which are beyond it," the mathematician Blaise Pascal wrote in the seventeenth century. "It is merely feeble if it does not go as far as to realize that. If natural things are beyond it, what are we to say about supernatural things?"

For the thoughtful believer, then, there is nothing more certain than the reality of uncertainty, nothing more natural than doubt, which is perhaps thirty seconds younger than faith itself. (And even that approximation may be giving faith too much of a head start.) "Our knowledge is imperfect," Paul wrote, "and our prophecy is imperfect." We live in twilight more than we do in clarity. Fundamentalist believers and fundamentalist atheists would both do well, I think, to acknowledge that literalism may be comforting but is ultimately dangerous, for an uncritical acceptance of one worldview or another (whether in religion or politics) ends more conversations than it begins. Light can neither emanate from, nor enter into, a closed mind. And so for all its limitations, reason—the weighing of evidence, the assessment of likelihood, the capacity to shift one's opinions in light of thought and of experience—remains essential. Without reason, we cannot appreciate complexity; without appreciating complexity, we cannot rightly appreciate the majesty and mystery of God; and without rightly appreciating the majesty and mystery of God, we foreclose the possibility of the miraculous and the redemptive.

The Christian story that began among a handful of Jews and worked its way out to the Mediterranean world to Rome and beyond is an archetypal one. There was once a world of light and harmony (in this case, in Eden). That world has fallen into evil hands and suffers under the sway of what Paul later called "principalities and powers." Jesus is the rescuer and hero who sacrifices all for the sake of the many in order to restore the rightful reign of the good and the just. In his Passion and resurrection, Jesus defeats death itself—the consummate victory.

But that is theology, an arena of debate and dissension without end. Let us begin with what is less subject to dispute. As a matter of history, we can stipulate that Jesus of Nazareth lived in Judea, undertook a mission of several years to his countrymen in which he preached the coming of the Kingdom of God (or "of heaven," which meant the same thing), ran afoul of both the Temple priests and the Roman rulers, and was executed by crucifixion during the commemoration of Passover in Jerusalem in about the year 33 C.E.

## FROM JESUS TO CHRIST

Convicted of sedition, condemned to death, nailed to a cross on a hill called Golgotha, he had endured all that he could. With a final, wordless cry, Jesus died. In the chaos of the arrest and crucifixion, his early followers had scattered. They had expected victory, not defeat, in this Jerusalem spring. If Jesus were, as they believed, the Jewish messiah, then his great achievement would have been the inauguration of God's Kingdom on earth, the restoration of the people of Israel, the resurrection of the dead, and the dawn of a new age marked by the end of evil and by the reign of justice, twin hallmarks of God's sovereignty.

The expected kingdom was a theme threading through the Jewish scriptures. According to the prophet Isaiah, there would one day be an hour of reckoning and reconciliation:

*The wilderness and the dry land shall be glad; the desert shall*
    *rejoice and blossom like the crocus;*
*it shall blossom abundantly and rejoice with joy and*
    *singing. . . .*
*They shall see the glory of the Lord, the majesty of our God.*
*Strengthen the weak hands, and make firm the feeble*
    *knees.*
*Say to those who have an anxious heart, "Be strong; fear not!*
*Behold, your God will come with vengeance,*
*with the recompense of God. He will come and save you."*
*Then the eyes of the blind shall be opened, and the ears of the*
    *deaf unstopped;*
*then shall the lame man leap like a deer, and the tongue of*
    *the mute sing for joy.*
*For waters break forth in the wilderness, and streams in the*
    *desert;*
*the burning sand shall become a pool, and the thirsty ground*
    *springs of water. . . .*
*And a highway shall be there, and it shall be called the Way*
    *of Holiness;*
*the unclean shall not pass over it. It shall belong to those who*
    *walk on the way; even if they are fools, they shall not go*
    *astray.*
*No lion shall be there, nor shall any ravenous beast come up*
    *on it;*
*they shall not be found there, but the redeemed shall walk*
    *there.*
*And the ransomed of the Lord shall return and come to Zion*
    *with singing;*

*everlasting joy shall be upon their heads; they shall obtain*
*gladness and joy, and sorrow and sighing shall flee away.*

Isaiah went on to elaborate on this vision of a restored order:

*How beautiful upon the mountains are the feet of him who*
*brings good news,*
*who publishes peace, who brings good news of happiness,*
*who publishes salvation, who says to Zion, "Your God*
*reigns."*
*The voice of your watchmen—they lift up their voice; to-*
*gether they sing for joy;*
*for eye to eye they see the return of the Lord to Zion.*
*Break forth together into singing, you waste places of*
*Jerusalem, for the Lord has comforted his people;*
*he has redeemed Jerusalem.*
*The Lord has bared his holy arm before the eyes of all the*
*nations,*
*and all the ends of the earth shall see the salvation of*
*our God.*

Or consider Psalm 98:

*O sing unto the Lord a new song; for he hath done marvel-*
*lous things: his right hand, and his holy arm, hath gotten*
*him the victory.*
*The Lord hath made known his salvation: his righteousness*
*hath he openly shewed in the sight of the heathen.*
*He hath remembered his mercy and his truth toward the*
*house of Israel: all the ends of the earth have seen the sal-*
*vation of our God.*

*Make a joyful noise unto the Lord, all the earth: make a loud
    noise, and rejoice, and sing praise.*
*Sing unto the Lord with the harp; with the harp, and the
    voice of a psalm.*
*With trumpets and sound of cornet make a joyful noise be-
    fore the Lord, the King.*
*Let the sea roar, and the fulness thereof; the world, and they
    that dwell therein.*
*Let the floods clap their hands: let the hills be joyful together*
*Before the Lord; for he cometh to judge the earth: with righ-
    teousness shall he judge the world, and the people with
    equity.*

But none of this came about on Good Friday. Instead, just as his followers were looking for the arrival
of God's kingdom on earth, Jesus seemed to have sung
no new song—or at least no song anyone else understood. Far from leading the forces of light to triumph,
he instead died an ignoble death. For the Roman authorities in Judea and for the Temple aristocrats concerned with placating the imperial officials, the political
implications of the "kingdom" were potentially dire.

In *Jesus of Nazareth, King of the Jews,* the scholar Paula
Fredriksen examines the Passion narrative in historical
terms. As best one can at such a distance, she seeks to
return us to the fraught hours of that Jerusalem Passover. It was Pontius Pilate, the Roman governor, who
was in control—not, as anti-Semitic sentiment would
have it, the Jewish high priests—and he was determined to keep order in the city amid the emotions and

the crowds of the Passover season. The kingdom, it seemed, was believed to be at hand. Perhaps Jesus had preached that this was the last Passover before the triumph of God's rule: "This news would have spread throughout the movement's human network," Fredriksen wrote, "linking villages from the Galilee through Judea and up to Jerusalem. Pilgrims gathering in the city for Passover, hearing the news in advance of Jesus's own arrival, consequently greeted him, when he appeared, as the human agent of God's coming kingdom—perhaps, indeed, as its king." He turned over the tables in the Temple; he seemed to be promising not a conventional Passover but a cataclysmic one.

The resulting outpouring of religious enthusiasm, with its attendant civil unrest and threat to the existing order, would have been the last thing Pilate needed. He was uninterested in theological disputes among the Jews; his task was to keep his territory in check. As the Jewish historian Josephus wrote, it was "on these festive occasions that sedition is most apt to break out." The elements for chaos were all there. "Jesus teaches in the Temple courtyard; the excited pilgrim crowds collect there," Fredriksen writes. "In the intensity of their expectation—that the kingdom was literally about to arrive? That Jesus was about to be revealed as messiah? That the restoration of Israel was at hand?—they are restive, potentially incendiary." The Temple elite worried about popular chaos, and unrest was anathema to both the entrenched religious authorities and to the governing Romans.

Thus Pilate sentenced Jesus to death. Crucifixion was the most public kind of execution, with the cross as a vivid warning not to challenge Rome. On the Friday of Passover, Fredriksen writes, "the pilgrim throng would have streamed out of the city to the hill just outside, to the Place of the Skull, Golgotha. There they would have beheld the man, dying on a cross. . . . As far as Pilate was concerned, that was the end of the matter."

But of course it wasn't. The early believers were looking for history to draw to a close—soon. Why else were the gospels written decades after the Passion? Could it be because Jesus's followers did not expect to need documents to pass on to ensuing generations because they believed that they were the *last* generation? "For the Lord himself shall descend from heaven with a shout, with the voice of the archangel . . . and the dead in Christ shall rise first," Paul wrote in First Thessalonians. "Then we which are alive and remain shall be caught up together with them in the clouds, to meet the Lord in the air: and so shall we ever be with the Lord." If Jesus were returning to rule in a new kind of reality, there would be no need for biographies, for he would be right there, having just descended with a shout. As the years passed, however, and the kingdom did not come, the early Christians composed the gospels to capture the stories and traditions in anticipation of a much longer wait—and to make the case for their "good news" to the broader world.

The cross had led to the empty tomb, and the empty

tomb led to a Christian vision of a new order. After he died, Jesus was wrapped in a linen shroud and placed in a tomb carved out of the rock of a hillside. A stone sealed the grave and, according to Mark, just after the sun rose two days later, Mary Magdalene and two other women were on their way to anoint the corpse with spices. Their concerns were practical, ordinary: Would they have enough strength to move the stone aside? As they drew near, however, they saw that the tomb was already open. Puzzled, they went inside, and a young man in a white robe—not Jesus—sitting on the right side of the tomb said: "Do not be amazed; you seek Jesus of Nazareth, who was crucified. He has risen, he is not here; see the place where they laid him." Absorbing these words, the women, Mark says, "went out and fled from the tomb; for trembling and astonishment had come upon them."

And so begins the story of Christianity—with confusion, not with clarity; with mystery, not with certainty. According to Luke's Gospel, the disciples at first treated the women's report of the empty tomb as "an idle tale, and . . . did not believe them"; the Gospel of John says that Jesus's followers "as yet . . . did not know . . . that he must rise from the dead."

Without the crucifixion and the belief in his resurrection, it is virtually impossible to imagine that the Jesus movement would have long endured. A small band of devotees might have kept his name alive for a time, even insisting on his messianic identity by calling him Christ, but the group would have been just one of many sects in first-century Judaism, a world roiled and crushed by the war with Rome from 66 to 73—a conflict that resulted in the destruction of Jerusalem.

So how, exactly, did the Jesus of history, whom many in his own time saw as a failed prophet, come to be viewed by billions as the Christ of faith whom the Nicene Creed says is "the only-begotten Son of God . . . God of God, Light of Light, Very God of very God . . . by whom all things were made"?

As the sun set on the Friday of the execution, Jesus appeared to be a disappointment, his promises about the Kingdom of God little more than provocative but powerless rhetoric. No matter what Jesus may have said about sacrifice and resurrection during his lifetime, the disciples clearly did not expect Jesus to rise again. The women at the tomb on Sunday were stunned; told that the Lord had risen, Thomas refused to believe until he saw Jesus for himself; and at the end of Matthew's Gospel, some disciples still "doubted."

Jesus can be confounding, and he forced the early believers to become masters of theological improvisation. First the kingdom failed to materialize at the time of the Passion. Next came the initially mystifying resurrection. Then came . . . nothing.

Prevailing Jewish tradition did not suggest that God would restore Israel and inaugurate the kingdom through a condemned man who went meekly to his death. Yet a sacrificial, atoning role is the one the first followers of Jesus ultimately believed he had played in the world. Where did this interpretation of his mission—one that emerged by the time Paul was writing his epistles in the decades after the Passion—come from? Perhaps from recollections of the words of Jesus himself. The apostles had to arrive at their definition of his messianic mission somehow, and Jesus likely spoke of these things during his lifetime—words that came flooding back to his followers after the Passion. On historical grounds, then, Christianity is a faith derived in part from oral or written traditions dating from the time of Jesus's ministry and that of his disciples. "The Son of man is delivered into the hands of men, and they shall kill him; and after that . . . he shall rise the third day," Jesus says in Mark, who adds that the disciples at the time "understood not that saying, and were afraid to ask him."

That the apostles would have created such words and ideas out of thin air seems unlikely, for their story and their message strained credulity even then. Paul admitted the difficulty: "But we preach Christ crucified, unto the Jews a stumblingblock, and unto the Greeks foolishness." A king who died a slave's death? A human atoning sacrifice? A resurrected messiah? As Paul asserted in one of the earliest known writings in the New Testament, however, the heart of the matter was just that: Jesus "gave himself for our sins, that he might deliver us from this present evil world, according to the will of God and our Father." Why invent something with no historical basis in the preaching of Jesus himself? The Christian salvation story was singular and specific, offering a peculiar religious riff on the extant symphony of Judaism. That the disciples understood Jesus so poorly at the time of the Passion is evidence of the power and prevalence of the existing theology of God's Kingdom, a theology that anticipated an imminent final struggle between the forces of good and evil.

In writing the gospels, and then in formulating church doctrine in the second, third, and fourth centuries, Jesus's followers reacted to his failure to return by reinterpreting their theological views in light of their historical experience. If the kind of kingdom they had so long expected was not at hand, then Jesus's life, death, and resurrection must have meant something different. The Christ they had looked for in the beginning was not the Christ they had come to know. His kingdom was not literally arriving, but he had, they came to believe, created something new: the church, the sacraments, the promise of salvation at the last day—whenever that might be.

The shift of emphasis from the short to the long term was an essential achievement. Because the early believers became convinced that Jesus's Passion and resurrection had given them the keys to heaven, they cared less about the hour of his coming, for God was worth the wait. Drawing on imagery in Isaiah, John the Divine evoked the ultimate glory in the Book of Revelation: "And God shall wipe away all tears from their eyes; and there shall be no more death, neither sorrow, nor crying, neither shall there be any more pain: for the former things are passed away. And he that sat upon the throne said, Behold, I make all things new."

Jesus's words at the Last Supper—that bread and wine represented his body and blood—now made more sense: He was, the early church argued, a sacrificial lamb in the tradition of ancient Israel. Turning to the old scriptures, the apostles began to find what they decided were prophecies Jesus had fulfilled. Hitting upon the fifty-third chapter of Isaiah, they interpreted the crucifixion as a necessary portal to a yet more glorious day: "He was wounded for our transgressions, he was bruised for our iniquities . . . and with his stripes we are healed." Jesus's followers saw their risen Lord as a figure foreseen in passages like this one from Daniel: "I saw in the night visions, and behold, with the clouds of heaven there came one like a son of man, and he came to the Ancient of Days and was presented before him. And to him was given dominion and glory and a kingdom, that all peoples, nations, and languages should serve him; his dominion is an everlasting dominion, which shall not pass away, and his kingdom one that shall not be destroyed."

To be sure, anyone reading the ancient Israelite texts outside the Christian tradition may not necessarily interpret them as prologue to the New Testament; the biblical books have their own histories and tell their own stories. To think Christianity negates God's covenant with Israel, meanwhile, is misguided and contrary to canonical teaching. During the Second

Vatican Council, the Roman Catholic Church issued an important document, *Nostra Aetate* ("In Our Time"), that argued against anti-Semitism and made the case for respecting differing faiths: "The Church reproves, as foreign to the mind of Christ, any discrimination against men or harassment of them because of their race, color, condition of life, or religion." God's choice of the Jewish people, Paul wrote, is eternal: "As regards election, they are beloved for the sake of their fore-fathers. . . . The gifts and the calling of God are irrevocable."

Whatever one thinks of Christianity, Jesus gave birth to a lasting vision of the origins, nature, and destiny of human life, a vision drawn from the religion's deep roots in Judaism. Everyone is created in God's image; there is, as Paul said, "neither Jew nor Greek, there is neither slave nor free, there is no male and female, for you are all one in Christ Jesus"; all are equal, precious, worthy. Humility was essential; generosity, vital; love, central. And the message was so powerful, so enveloping, that the notion of God's manifesting himself in human form and subjecting himself to pain and death inspired martyrdom and suffering. Writing about Rome under Nero, Tacitus reported that Christians "were covered in the skins of wild animals, torn to death by dogs, crucified or set on fire—so that when darkness fell they burned like torches in the night."

So many theological questions linger, and always will: Did Jesus understand his relationship to God the Father in the way Christians now do? Luke claims he did: "The Son of man must suffer many things, and be rejected," Jesus says, "and be slain, and be raised the third day." Did he grasp his atoning role? John claims he did: "I am the living bread which came down from heaven: if any man eat of this bread, he shall live forever: and the bread that I will give is my flesh, which I will give for the life of the world." But how much of this is remembered history, and how much heartfelt but unhistorical theology? It is impossible to say. "How unsearchable are his judgments," Paul writes of the Lord, "and how inscrutable his ways!"

Unless and until we come, in Paul's words, "face to face" with God, we are left with an exhortation from a favorite text of Saint Augustine's, the 105th Psalm: "Seek the Lord, and his strength: seek his face evermore." As the search goes on for so many along so many different paths, Paul offered some guidance for the journey: "Be at peace among yourselves. . . . Encourage the fainthearted, help the weak, be patient with them all. See that none of you repays evil for evil, but always seek to do good to one another and to all. Rejoice always, pray constantly, give thanks . . . hold fast what is good, abstain from every form of evil"—wise words for all of us, whatever our doubts, whatever our faith.

## THE WONDROUS CROSS

But we are getting ahead of our story. Before we can celebrate the mystery of Easter and consider the origins of Christian doctrine, we must contemplate the misery of Good Friday.

Jesus hung on a cross that was probably about six to eight feet high; crosses did not loom high over Jerusalem as they so often do in the art of the Middle Ages. He not only died as one of us; he died among us. The question for us is what it meant, and what it means. Put in Pilate's terms: What was, and what *is,* the truth of the cross?

History is what happened in time and space. Theology can be understood as what people think history means in relation to a presumed order beyond time and space. History is horizontal, theology vertical, and their intersection is a motive force behind our religious, national, and personal imaginations. The stories we tell ourselves about who we are, what we love, and how we live are furnished and fired by the factual and the fabled. History and theology are inextricably bound up with each other, and together, I submit, they create truth. Fact is what we can see or discern; truth is the larger significance we extrapolate from those facts.

So it was on Golgotha two millennia ago. The Last Words are at once history and theology. Appreciating that we come to the story of Jesus seeing in two dimensions, on two levels, will make our work together easier. Christian faith is binocular. The Passion was both a historical event that unfolded in Jerusalem and a theological event that transformed the world. Those at the foot of the cross could see and hear Jesus, but what they were seeing and hearing was not the whole story. Jesus cried out to God; his followers heard the cries; what the audience could not know then was that the Jesus of history was about to become the Christ of faith, an intersection of the visible and the invisible that would alter how innumerable souls understand reality.

To ponder the Seven Last Words does not require us to take the gospel accounts as literal reports, as though we're reading about the invasion of Normandy or the Cuban missile crisis. I think that it is more illuminating to treat the gospel claims about the last hours of Jesus on earth as clues to the hopes and fears of the faithful as they struggled to make sense of that tumultuous Friday.

As we will see, the gospel authors—the sources for the Last Words—were not writing history as we tend to think of it. "It is not that the sources are in themselves bad," Albert Schweitzer wrote in the early twentieth century. "When we have once made up our minds that we have not the materials for a complete Life of Jesus, but only for a picture of His public ministry, it must be admitted that there are few characters of antiquity about whom we possess so much indubitably historical information, of whom we have so many authentic discourses. The position is much more favorable, for instance, than in the case of Socrates."

Still, the gospels are not biographies but apologetic documents, composed to persuade, to inspire, and to convince. (John is explicit about this: "These are written that you may believe . . . and that believing you may have life in his name.") The gospels must be read critically, with a sense of historical context. Which is to say, the Last Words that we are about to encounter may or may not have actually been spoken by Jesus. What is certain is that each of the evangelists thought it important for his audience to *believe* that Jesus had said them.

That leads us to the devotional nature of the current project. We are not here to assess the historicity of each of the Last Words; we are here, instead, to use these sayings as the occasion to offer some thoughts about Good Friday, about the origins of the faith, and about its implications and applications for those intrigued by the story of the cross and the unfolding story of Christianity.

The short essays that follow were originally conceived and drafted for delivery at the Three Hours Devotion at the Episcopal parish of St. Thomas Church Fifth Avenue in New York City on Good Friday. The custom of reflecting on Jesus's reported words from the cross—seven brief but epochal remarks gathered together from the gospels—dates at least from the Middle Ages. In 1618, Saint Robert Bellarmine, an Italian Jesuit, published *The Seven Last Words from the Cross.* To Bellarmine, the cross was "the pulpit of the Preacher, the altar of the Sacrificing Priest, the arena of the Combatant, the workshop of the Wonder-worker"; Jesus's words, Bellarmine wrote, should be seen (and heard) as "the last sermon which the Redeemer of the world preached . . . as from an elevated pulpit, to the human race." The Last Words have inspired composers (Haydn's eighteenth-century work is perhaps the most celebrated), writers (John Donne, Gerard Manley Hopkins, and James Joyce, among others), and preachers. The collection of sayings gives us occasion to turn not only our hearts but our minds toward the cross—an opportunity to *think* as well as *feel,* especially on the darkest of days, Good Friday.

Just before he goes to the Garden of Gethsemane on the eve of his death, Jesus, according to the Gospel of John, "lifted up his eyes to heaven, and said, Father, the hour is come." The shadows are lengthening and the Passion is at hand—the betrayal, the arrest, the scourging, the crucifixion, the gasping, and, at last, the death.

For Christians, the coming of Jesus's hour is the hinge of history. With Jesus we are not fantasists but keepers of a witnessed tradition, and our faith is rooted in the testimony of apostles and prophets, of evangelists and martyrs, of saints and scholars. I say this as a believer, yes, but I also say it as a historian who spends his days sifting through the chaos of the past in a quest to understand, however provisionally and however partially, how and why we came to be the people we are.

We stand now at the cross, in the moments of Jesus's greatest pain. May we bear in mind the central emotional truth of Good Friday: that the Christian tradition grew from the most wrenching, mysterious, and mystifying sacrifice imaginable—that of a father's offering of his child. We kneel before the cross in homage to self-giving love, and the cross should serve as both rebuke and reminder—a rebuke to the world for its vanities and sins, and a reminder that at the center of the Christian story lies love, not hate; grace, not rage; mercy, not vengeance. That is at least one answer to Pilate's question about truth.

# THE FIRST WORD

And there were also two other, malefactors, led with him
to be put to death. And when they were come to the place,
which is called Calvary, there they crucified him, and the
malefactors, one on the right hand, and the other on the left.
Then said Jesus,

## *Father, forgive them; for they know not what they do.*

And they parted his raiment, and cast lots. And the people
stood beholding. And the rulers also with them derided him,
saying, He saved others; let him save himself,
if he be Christ, the chosen of God.
And the soldiers also mocked him, coming to him,
and offering him vinegar,
And saying, If thou be the king of the Jews,
save thyself.
And a superscription also was written over him
in letters of Greek, and Latin, and Hebrew,
This Is The King Of The Jews.

—LUKE 23:32–38

J ESUS'S FIRST REMARK FROM THE CROSS is found exclusively in Luke: "Father, forgive them, for they know not what they do." It's fitting that the first word should be as problematic as this one is, for the drama of the cross is itself mysterious.

Let us briefly recapitulate what we know about the road to Golgotha. Born to Mary, a young woman, Jesus preached the coming of the Kingdom of God, a kingdom that would unseat the temporal powers of the world and bring about a universal acknowledgment of Israel's God. "Repent," he said, "for the kingdom of heaven is at hand." In Mark, likely the earliest gospel, Jesus was reported to have foretold coming chaos, and then order:

> And when ye shall hear of wars and rumors of wars, be ye not troubled: for such things must needs be; but the end shall not be yet.
> For nation shall rise against nation, and kingdom against kingdom: and there shall be earthquakes in divers places, and there shall be famines and troubles: these are the beginnings of sorrows. . . .

> In those days, after that tribulation, the sun shall be dark-
> ened, and the moon shall not give her light,
> And the stars of heaven shall fall, and the powers that are in
> heaven shall be shaken.
> And then shall they see the Son of man coming in the
> clouds. . . .
> And then shall he send his angels, and shall gather together
> his elect from the four winds, from the uttermost part of
> the earth to the uttermost part of heaven. . . .
> Verily I say unto you, that this generation shall not pass, till
> all these things be done.

In his public ministry, Jesus attracted devout followers. Performing miraculous deeds, he appeared to
cure the sick, exorcise demons, and even raise the dead.
The reports of his triumphant entry into Jerusalem in
the week before his final Passover suggest that he was
embraced enthusiastically by Jewish pilgrims to the
holy city—and was thus seen as a destabilizing force by
Jerusalem's ruling authorities. (Jesus was executed in
the wake of anti-Roman activity bloody enough to
have resulted in the conviction of at least three other
men, including Barabbas, whom the gospels tell us was
being held for execution for his role in that violent ep-
isode.) It was, then, a time of tumult and of uncertainty,
and, historically speaking, the crucifixion was probably
the result of ecstatic crowds looking to Jesus to bring
the kingdom to earth *right then.*

If Jesus had truly been a revolutionary threat in the
traditional sense of leading or inspiring an armed up-

rising, he would most likely not have been the only figure from his circle to die. His followers were left alone in the aftermath of the crucifixion and were free, in the fullness of time, to settle in Jerusalem as they worked out a new understanding of what Jesus's death on the cross and his empty tomb meant. Complex matters, and big themes—the biggest, really, one can conceive of. And why not? The Christian undertaking, derived from its roots in Judaism, is about a cosmology that attempts to account for the seeming triumphs of evil and asserts the conviction that justice and goodness will prevail. *Of course* it's complicated.

The Seven Last Words are collected from the different gospel accounts as a devotional exercise, and the church has long chosen to begin its Good Friday services with Jesus's words of absolution. Yet my sense is that we take the wrong lesson from Jesus's declaration of forgiveness if we read it—as many preachers do—as an affirmation of the wideness of God's mercy. Look, sermon after sermon has asserted, look at the amazing grace of Jesus; even in the starkest of pain and in the most exquisite of agonies, the Son of man embraces all sinners, extending salvation to the torturers who are in the midst of murdering him.

True, the theme of forgiveness is a strong element in Luke's Gospel and beyond. (Dante would refer to Luke as "the scribe of the gentleness of Christ.") Earlier it is Luke who recounts Jesus's teaching to "Love your enemies, do good to those who hate you, bless those who curse you, pray for those who mistreat you."

Later, in Acts, Luke writes of Saint Stephen's similar prayer that the Lord forgive those who persecute him. Another ancient source claims that in the early sixties, James, the brother of the Lord, prayed, "Lord, God, Father, forgive them, for they do not know what they are doing" as those in a rival party stoned him.

It's tempting, then, to interpret Jesus's own words of forgiveness from the cross as an embodiment of his mission of mercy to the world. Here, though, is the problem as I see it: If God's plan required his Son's death and resurrection, then why would the agents of that plan require absolution? We are taught that Jesus had to die as a ransom for many. Without his suffering, death, and resurrection, then there would be no salvation, no new heaven and new earth. Nowhere in the New Testament does anyone argue that Jesus could accomplish the work of redemption by living out a natural life and dying gently in his sleep deeper into the first century. No, the story is the opposite: Jesus was to submit obediently to the will of the Father, who had decreed that his Son would die a violent death so that all might one day be forgiven their sins and granted eternal life.

Standing as we do so many centuries removed from the events we commemorate in Holy Week, let us be clear: Jesus's death was essential to Christian hope. So why does Luke have Jesus seem to be forgiving his tormentors for playing the critical and necessary role in bringing about the salvation of the world and the coming of a kingdom of justice?

The answer may lie in the cares and concerns of the gospel writer himself. We should put ourselves as far back as we can into the decades following Jesus's Passion. Our gospels were composed forty to seventy years after Jesus's death. Each was written with certain audiences and particular communities in mind. Some themes are underscored, some downplayed, depending on those whom the evangelist is trying to reach and to convince. Seen in this light, Luke's inclusion of the "Father, forgive them, for they know not what they do" line is a mark of rhetorical genius. Any Gentile hearing the story in that Roman-dominated world could feel exculpated, for the imperial authorities were being exculpated, enabling the Gentile audience to put away its anxieties about its complicity in the murder. Any Jew hearing the story could also feel exculpated; the Temple establishment had done what it had done, but here was Jesus himself, in Luke's rendering, forgiving the sin.

It is illogical to hold either the Romans or the Temple establishment as in any sense "guilty" for the death of a Savior whose suffering was foreordained and whose mission inaugurated a salvation history that shall wipe away every human tear. We, however, are coming to the story—and to the cross—with the benefit of centuries of theological reflection. For those first generations of Jesus's followers, the saga of the Lord's ministry and Passion was paradoxical and confusing. It can be even yet, for the work of the cross marks a radical departure from ordinary human experience.

The task of the evangelists—the task of Luke—was to bring as many souls into the fold as possible at a time when the Christian movements were tenuous and fragile. By reporting that Jesus himself had forgiven all those who might be blamed for his brutal death, Luke was making the faith more accessible and appealing than it might have otherwise been. There was world enough and time for talk of nuances like the ones we are discussing now. In the rough-and-tumble of the first century or two, a time of political strife and social upheaval, best to cast the widest net possible.

Luke was particularly skilled at this complicated task: His gospel, as well as his volume the Acts of the Apostles, is a literary epic. It is Luke who gives us, for example, the *Magnificat* ("My soul doth magnify the Lord, And my spirit hath rejoiced in God my Saviour") and the *Benedictus* ("Blessed be the Lord God of Israel, for he hath visited and redeemed his people; And hath raised up a horn of salvation for us in the house of his servant David; As he spake by the mouth of his holy prophets, which have been since the world began: That we should be saved from our enemies, and from the hand of all that hate us"). He writes of epiphanies, of the revelation of Jesus to the greater world. In Luke's hands, Jesus's role as savior is first proclaimed:

And there were in the same country shepherds abiding in the field, keeping watch over their flock by night. And, lo, the angel of the Lord came upon them, and the glory of the Lord shone round about them: and they were sore afraid. And the angel said unto them, Fear not: for, behold, I bring you good tidings of great joy, which shall be to all people. For unto you is born this day in the city of David a Saviour, which is Christ the Lord. And this shall be a sign unto you; Ye shall find the babe wrapped in swaddling clothes, lying in a manger. And suddenly there was with the angel a multitude of the heavenly host praising God, and saying, Glory to God in the highest, and on earth peace, good will toward men.

My good friend and sometime rector Andrew Mead tells a story about the great classical scholar Richmond Lattimore, a poet and noted translator of Greek, including the New Testament. A professor at Bryn Mawr College near Philadelphia, Lattimore regularly attended Mass with his wife at the Episcopal Church of the Good Shepherd in Rosemont. He never came to the altar rail for Holy Communion, however, and Father Mead thought, rightly, that Lattimore was a skeptic. And yet, late in life, Lattimore agreed to be baptized.

"Dr. Lattimore," Andrew asked, "I thought you had reservations about the Christian faith and the church."

"I did," Lattimore replied.

"But you don't any longer?"

"No, not any longer."

"Please, then, may I ask you, when did they go away?"

"Somewhere in Saint Luke."

*Somewhere in Saint Luke:* The gospel that began with the drama of a child's conception and in many ways climaxes at Golgotha and in the garden tomb where Jesus had been buried but rose again told a story of such power that its purpose—the conversion of the wider world—was still unfolding nearly two thousand years later. "Heaven and earth shall pass away," Jesus says in Luke, "but my words shall not pass away."

My reading of the First Word is a critical one, if by "critical" one means interpretative rather than literal. In this I am following in an ancient exegetical tradition, one that holds the scriptures to be perhaps inspired but certainly fallible. We are called to use our minds as well as our hearts in reading the Bible, deciding, through the use of reason, whether a given passage is an actual report or a theological device. The Bible was not FedExed from heaven, nor did the Lord God of Hosts send a pdf or a link to scripture. Written in Greek, and drawing on a Greek translation of originally Hebrew scriptures, the gospels tell stories in a language foreign to Jesus himself. We must engage with the texts of the faith with reason, a critical intelligence, and a capacity to distinguish history from legend, narrative from allegory, and fact from apologetics.

This is not a widely popular view, for it transforms the "Jesus loves me / Yes I know / for the Bible tells me so" ethos of Sunday schools and vacation Bible camps into something more challenging. A few years ago I was with a group of clergy on the East Coast. The conversation turned to critical interpretations of the New

Testament. I remarked that I did not see how people could make sense of the Bible if they were taught to think of it as a collection of ancient Associated Press reports. (CANA, GALILEE—*In a surprise development yesterday at a local wedding, Jesus of Nazareth transformed water into wine.*) "That's your critical reading of the gospels," one minister replied, "but in the pulpit I can't do that." Why? I asked. "Because," he said, "you can't mess with Jesus."

The objecting cleric's remark illuminated one of the issues facing not only Christians but also the broader world: To what extent should holy books be read and interpreted critically rather than taken literally? To later generations of the faithful, what was written in fluctuating circumstances can assume the status of immutable fact.

It's certainly true that for the searcher or the believer, the point of reading sacred writings is not the same as reading, say, the history of the Punic Wars or of World War II. The texts are directive documents. As the Second Epistle of Timothy says, "All Scripture is God-breathed and is useful for teaching, rebuking, correcting and training in righteousness, so that the servant of God may be thoroughly equipped for every good work."

Fair enough, and Saint Augustine echoed the point, writing, "Whoever thinks he has understood the divine scriptures or any part of them in such a way that his understanding does not build up the twin love of God and neighbor has not yet understood them at all."

Yet context and criticism matter. "To search out the intention of the sacred writers, attention should be given, among other things, to 'literary forms,'" the Roman Catholic Church wrote in a 1965 document, *Dei Verbum*. "For truth is set forth and expressed differently in texts which are variously historical, prophetic, poetic, or of other forms of discourse. . . . For the correct understanding of what the sacred author wanted to assert, due attention must be paid to the customary and characteristic styles of feeling, speaking and narrating which prevailed at the time of the sacred writer, and to the patterns men normally employed at that period in their everyday dealings with one another."

The first word we hear from the cross, then, is a reminder that all we are to hear is not to be taken uncritically. In a prayer published in the 1549 English Book of Common Prayer, scripture is, rather, to be heard, read, marked, learned, and inwardly digested with care and an appreciation of context. Reason and faith are the wings with which we can rise from the darkness of ignorance and despair, seeking forgiveness and nothing less than holiness in a profane world. And "Somewhere in Saint Luke" is not a bad place to begin.

# THE
# SECOND WORD

———

*Then one of the criminals who were hanged blasphemed
Him, saying, "If You are the Christ, save Yourself and us."
But the other, answering, rebuked him, saying, "Do you
not even fear God, seeing you are under the same
condemnation? And we indeed justly, for we receive the
due reward of our deeds; but this Man has done nothing
wrong." Then he said to Jesus, "Lord, remember me
when You come into Your kingdom."
And Jesus said to him,*

## "Assuredly, I say to you, today
## you will be with Me in Paradise."

—LUKE 23:39–43

E VEN BY THE HARSH STANDARDS of the ancient world, crucifixion was brutal. To Rome, which reserved it especially to discourage rebellions against the imperial order, the *crux* was the supreme punishment, the most vicious and demeaning of the tripartite *summa supplicia* (the second was being burned alive, the third— used for upper-class offenders and for citizens—was decapitation). "Can any man be found willing to be fastened to the accursed tree, long sickly, already deformed, swelling with ugly weals on shoulders and chest, and drawing the breath of life amid long-drawn-out agony?" the Roman Stoic Seneca wrote. "He would have many excuses for dying even before mounting the cross."

To weaken the condemned, soldiers would scourge him. "The usual instrument was a short whip . . . with several single or braided leather thongs of variable lengths, in which small iron balls or sharp pieces of sheep bones were tied at intervals," the *Journal of the American Medical Association* reported in 1986. "Occasionally, staves also were used. For scourging, the man was stripped of his clothing, and his hands were tied to an upright post. The back, buttocks, and legs were flogged either by two soldiers (lictors) or by one who alternated positions. The severity of the scourging depended on the disposition of the lictors and was intended to weaken the victim to a state just short of collapse or death."

The condemned was typically forced to carry the horizontal crossbar, known as the patibulum, to the place of execution. This was an additional element of torture, for the patibulum tended to weigh between 75 and 125 pounds. He would be nailed to the finished cross—through the wrists more often than the palms—by "tapered iron spikes approximately 5 to 7 inches" long; similar nails would go through the feet. The crucified tended to die from asphyxiation and shock from blood loss. It is difficult to conceive of a slower and more painful way to die. Cicero referred to crucifixion, which was designed to be as public as possible in order to serve as a deterrent, as a "plague"; the scholar Martin Hengel believed it "satisfied the primitive lust for revenge and the sadistic cruelty of individual rulers. . . . By the public display of a naked victim at a prominent place—at a crossroads, in the theatre, on high ground, at the place of his crime—crucifixion also represented his uttermost humiliation."

We are told that two others—"criminals," in the King James translation; political brigands or insurgents in more accurate, modern ones—were killed with Jesus. One of the men calls out to Jesus asking to be remembered when the Lord comes into his kingdom; Jesus replies with an assurance of redemption and peace.

The words mark the culmination of the central work of Jesus's public ministry, which has been centered on the proclamation of a kingdom in which the last shall be first. The presence of the other two men also dramatizes the complexities of the political hour in which the Passion unfolds. There had been a recent rebellion—one during which Barabbas, who was released by Pilate instead of Jesus, committed sedition and murder—and here are yet two other insurgents who have caused enough trouble for Rome to crucify them.

There is much speculation about the political backstory of Jesus's crucifixion. Scenarios include the possibility that he was seen as a revolutionary determined to overthrow Roman rule by force. That Jesus was an exclusively political figure, however, seems unlikely. If he had been, it is hard to believe that he alone would have died. Rome would have targeted his immediate followers as well. Why not crucify at least a few of the disciples, none of whom were even arrested, if a full-scale revolt was thought to be in the offing? Moreover, it is doubtful that the gospel message would have spread as it did among the Gentiles of the Roman Empire had its central character been executed as a traitor in the traditional sense of the word. Jesus disturbed the political order, yes, but he did so, it seems, by preaching the arrival of a kingdom that transcended the ordinary understandings of statecraft and by attracting popular support among the Passover crowds in Jerusalem at the time of his death.

To me, the forgiveness of this sympathetic insurgent

underscores the mystery of Jesus's love and of the inscrutability of faith. When we are being honest with ourselves, we aren't all that comfortable with inscrutability. Most of us prefer certainty to uncertainty, clarity to riddles. We like to think that we have, if not all the answers, at least more answers than other people.

If anything, the account of Jesus's redemption of the insurgent at Golgotha should give anyone claiming to know the mind of God enormous pause. The exchange is touching, even intimate. And the term "Paradise" is drawn from a Persian word signifying a garden or an enclosed park. John the Divine was to use the same word in the Revelation, writing, "He that hath an ear, let him hear what the Spirit saith unto the churches; To him that overcometh will I give to eat of the tree of life, which is in the midst of the paradise of God." Jesus's promise to the insurgent is the gift of everything. And it is also his promise to us.

*Today you will be with Me in Paradise:* God is all-powerful and far beyond our control and our comprehension. His mercy is available to all, even if the ways and means of grace remain mysterious, veiled from our eyes and our understandings. Let us just pray that we, too, may one day dwell in communion with the Lord and all those whom he has chosen to forgive. For we will need that forgiveness and that grace every bit as much as the condemned man who had the wisdom to call out to Jesus. The question is whether we will have the courage and the humility to make the same plea.

# THE
# THIRD WORD

―――

*Now there stood by the cross of Jesus his mother,
and his mother's sister, Mary the wife of Cleophas,
and Mary Magdalene.
When Jesus therefore saw his mother, and the disciple
standing by, whom he loved, he saith unto his mother,*

## Woman, behold thy son!

*Then saith he to the disciple,*

## Behold thy mother!

*And from that hour that disciple took her
unto his own home.*

—JOHN 19:25–27

WHEN JESUS COMMENDS HIS MOTHER to the care of John the Beloved Disciple, he is, at one level, taking care of a bit of important housekeeping, arranging the world he is leaving as best he could. In a larger sense, he is leaving a model for his followers to love one another in the most profound and powerful of ways. And loving ourselves doesn't count.

Quite the opposite. A young woman once wrote John Henry Newman a letter seeking personal spiritual counsel. Newman's reply was pointed—probably unexpectedly so: "You think of yourself more than of [God]: rejoice that He has hold of you, submit when He fixes you."

This is a fundamental call to fix our eyes not inwardly, but outwardly, on one another and, ultimately, on the cross. Every hour we think of ourselves, of getting and spending, we not only lay waste to our own powers but cut ourselves off from the events of Good Friday and of Easter. And to cut ourselves off from those events is to fail to take advantage of all the possibilities of humanity and of all the possibilities of love.

The charge to John to care for Mary is a reminder

that we must be, as the Epistle of James put it, doers of the Word and not hearers only. The gospel injunction about how we are to conduct ourselves in this world is clear. As Jesus says in Matthew,

> Then the King will say to those at his right hand, "Come, O blessed of my Father, inherit the kingdom prepared for you from the foundation of the world; for I was hungry and you gave me food, I was thirsty and you gave me drink, I was a stranger and you welcomed me, I was naked and you clothed me, I was sick and you visited me, I was in prison and you came to me." Then the righteous will answer him, "Lord, when did we see thee hungry and feed thee, or thirsty and give thee drink? And when did we see thee a stranger and welcome thee, or naked and clothe thee? And when did we see thee sick or in prison and visit thee?" And the King will answer them, "Truly, I say to you, as you did it to one of the least of these my brethren, you did it to me."

The point is then underscored:

> Then he will say to those at his left hand, "Depart from me, you cursed, into the eternal fire prepared for the devil and his angels; for I was hungry and you gave me no food, I was thirsty and you gave me no drink, I was a stranger and you did not welcome me, naked and you did not clothe me, sick and in prison and you did not visit me."

Yet we must be mindful, too, that the mystery of the church is about both faith and works. To do good but to forgo belief in the efficacy of the cross is surely better than doing no good at all. The point of Good Friday, however, is that we are invited into a mode of life that offers us a new way of seeing both the temporal and the transcendent. The story of Jesus is a guide and a gate; it urges us to do unto each other as we would have others do unto us, and in so doing we are drawn ever closer to the cross—the emblem of unselfish love. We are free to decline the invitation, of course, and many do. But the invitation is still there, forever open. "Come and see," Jesus said to those who would become his disciples at the beginning of his ministry.

*Come and see:* Why not come and see? Why not, to borrow another image from the New Testament, take the advice that the Epistle to the Philippians offers here: "Finally, brethren, whatever is true, whatever is honorable, whatever is just, whatever is pure, whatever is lovely, whatever is gracious, if there is any excellence, if there is anything worthy of praise, think about these things."

After some thought, you may well find that the whole story is not something you can accept. So be it: You would be in excellent company. In a letter to Yale president Ezra Stiles just before his own death, the aged Benjamin Franklin wrote:

I believe in one God, creator of the universe. That he governs it by his providence. That he ought to be worshipped. That the most acceptable service we can render to him, is doing good to his other children. That the soul of man is immortal, and will be treated with justice in another life respecting its conduct in this. These I take to be the fundamental principles of all sound religion, and I regard them as you do, in whatever sect I meet with them. As to Jesus of Nazareth . . . I think the system of morals and his religion as he left them to us, the best the world ever saw, or is likely to see; but I apprehend it has received various corrupting changes, and I have . . . some doubts as to his divinity; though it is a question I do not dogmatise upon, having never studied it, and think it needless to busy myself with it now, when I expect soon an opportunity of knowing the truth with less trouble.

One hopes that worked out for Dr. Franklin. But the safer hope, I think, is to heed the old story we are told anew on Good Friday, accepting the testimony of the apostles and holding fast to the faith. Not blindly—for blind faith is not faith but fundamentalism—but reverently, respectfully, and joyfully. We should, with John, who accepts the charge to become a son to Mary, take care of one another, remembering always that it is through love that we glimpse the divine, and touch the cross of Christ.

# THE
# FOURTH WORD

---

*Now from the sixth hour there was darkness*
*over all the land unto the ninth hour.*
*And about the ninth hour Jesus cried with a loud voice,*
*saying, Eli, Eli, lama sabachthani? that is to say,*

## My God, my God,
## why hast thou forsaken me?

—MATTHEW 27:45–46

HERE, IN THE MIDDLE OF OUR JOURNEY, we come to the heart of the matter. Jesus's cry from Psalm 22 is the most human and resonant word of the afternoon. The word "cry" is significant, for "cry" or "shout" is usually used in the Bible as a great call to action—often redemptive, miraculous action. When Jesus raised Lazarus from the dead, he "cried with a loud voice, Lazarus, come forth." And remember we were told in First Thessalonians that "the Lord himself shall descend from heaven with a shout, with the voice of the archangel." Even the people of God—all of us— are instructed to shout to bring about a new order, for, as the psalmist advises:

> O clap your hands, all ye people; shout unto God with the
>     voice of triumph.
> For the Lord most high is terrible; he is a great King over all
>     the earth.
> He shall subdue the people under us, and the nations under
>     our feet.

Jesus's cry on the cross about being forsaken by the Father raises intriguing questions. If, as the faithful suppose—and as the gospels, in their Passion predictions, insist—Jesus was fully briefed on his earthly mission, then how could his cry be taken literally? Why ask whether God has forsaken him? Why cry in pain when he must have known that resurrection lay ahead?

We don't know. What we can say is this: Mark and Matthew have already told us that, at Gethsemane, Jesus asked that the cup pass from him but that the Father's will, not the Son's, should be done. In Mark and Matthew, then, Jesus is more of a tragic character than in Luke or John (which do not include the "My God, my God" word from the cross).

To me, this more human Jesus is a compelling figure, and I suspect Mark and Matthew thought so, too. By portraying him as one who would cry out in pain and in anguish, they make him more accessible, more understandable, more like *us*. The interpretative issue, the Roman Catholic scholar Raymond E. Brown wrote, "is whether the struggle with evil will lead to victory; and Jesus is portrayed as profoundly discouraged at the end of his long battle because God, to whose will Jesus committed himself at the beginning of the Passion, has not intervened in the struggle and seemingly has left Jesus unsupported. . . . Jesus cries out, hoping that God will break through the alienation he has felt." As a people whose lives are frequently defined by feelings of alienation—from one another *and* from the Creator—we recognize in Jesus what we ourselves suffer, thus drawing closer to the truth of the cross.

And that truth is grounded in history, for whatever we might think of the accuracy of the Last Words or of the sundry details of the crucifixion, we can safely say that Jesus of Nazareth really did suffer and really did die on a Roman cross. Such (along with the empty tomb) was the primary teaching of the oldest New Testament traditions—traditions that gave life and energy to the church that we know even now.

If he did not suffer, if he did not bleed, if he did not feel every bit of the pain of execution as he gulped for air, then he would not be the Christ we know. He was fulfilling his epochal role in history on that cross; he was not playacting, not a god pretending to die. He was the Word made flesh, who was, however strangely and incomprehensibly, full of grace and truth.

There is that word again, the word we first heard in the interview with Pilate: "truth." The Greek meaning of the term both from Pilate's lips and in the prologue of Saint John's Gospel is "unconcealed," or "real," as opposed to that which is mendacious or misleading.

The cry about being forsaken is as moving a moment as we find in the gospels, or in any work of ancient literature. It is important, too, for us to note that, read in its entirety, Psalm 22 is a journey from despair to hope. Listen to the latter part of the scripture Jesus invoked on the cross:

> *Deliver my soul from the sword; my darling from the power of the dog.*

*Save me from the lion's mouth. . . .*

*I will declare thy name unto my brethren: in the midst of the congregation will I praise thee.*

*Ye that fear the Lord, praise him; all ye the seed of Jacob, glorify him; and fear him, all ye the seed of Israel.*

*For he hath not despised nor abhorred the affliction of the afflicted; neither hath he hid his face from him; but when he cried unto him, he heard.*

*My praise shall be of thee in the great congregation. . . .*

*The meek shall eat and be satisfied: they shall praise the Lord that seek him: your heart shall live for ever.*

*All the ends of the world shall remember and turn unto the Lord: and all the kindreds of the nations shall worship before thee.*

*For the kingdom is the Lord's: and he is the governor among the nations.*

Light in the darkness, life from death, rescue from tribulation: such are the promises of Psalm 22, and, one supposes, of God the Father, through the momentary forsaking of the Son. It is hardly surprising that the rawest words of the crucifixion should perhaps tell us the most about the divine meaning of Golgotha, a place of violence and of hate transformed into a manifestation of indescribable *agape.*

When I am asked, as I occasionally am, how it is that I can believe in God, I answer as honestly and straightforwardly as I can. I believe in God on the same evidence that I believe in love: Both are invisible forces with visible effects. Sometimes these effects are noble, redemptive, warm, thrilling, and transporting; sometimes, when love goes wrong and turns to self-regard, or to jealousy, or finally to hate, then it produces corruption and disorder.

In my own life, whenever I fall short of the mark, or hurt someone, or do those things which I ought not to have done, I tend to do so because of the sin of pride, which is when love becomes self-regard, and my gaze, which is rightly directed outward, toward others, has turned inward, toward me, focusing not on what I should do but on the devices and desires of my own heart.

One way to set things right again is to return to Golgotha, and to the Lord of history and of love who died there. His story—of resurrection amid death and of love amid hate—gives hope to the fearful, redemption to the fallen, and order to chaos. And there can be no greater story than that.

It is a story about reversal. It is not about denying the realities of life, nor is it about escaping into a fairyland. It is, rather, about acknowledging the inevitability of crisis and affirming the hope of renewal. It is about enduring in the confidence that the truth of Jesus Christ shapes and suffuses life on earth and beyond.

Literalism is for the weak; fundamentalism is for the insecure. Both are sins, too, against God, for to come to believe that we are in exclusive possession of the truth about things *beyond* time and space, and thus hold the power to shape lives and decisions about things *within* time and space, is to put ourselves in the place of God. But we are taught that no man has searched the mind of the Lord, or been his counselor.

We are as enveloped in mystery as human beings have been since the first human fist was raised in anguish toward the sky, asking the most fundamental of questions: *Why?* Why do the innocent suffer, and the innocent die? Why are some rich, others poor? Why do some find love while others search fruitlessly and futilely, seeking a happiness that seems forever out of reach? Why are some hearts full, and others perpetually broken?

We do not know. The world is a tragic place: It will never finally, fully conform to our wishes.

Sometimes the things in front of us, including the cross, are the things we notice the least. We do not genuflect to images of an empty tomb, or of a discarded shroud. We genuflect, rather, to a representation of a place of suffering and of sweat, of blood and of death. Tragedy is ever before us. From the cross, Jesus asked the same question we ask in hours of darkness and despair: *My God, my God, why hast thou forsaken me?* God has thus known grief. He has experienced the pain of his people. He has wondered *why.*

Then his Father's will was done, and from darkness came light, and death was conquered. This is our story, our faith, our consolation.

And so we watch and we wait, revering the cross,

caring for the widow and the orphan, and holding fast to the belief that someday, in some way, all things shall be made new. For that hope is all we have to hold on to, however tenuously, in the hours when we, too, feel forsaken by the Father, and far from his care.

# THE FIFTH WORD

*After this, Jesus knowing that all things were now accomplished, that the scripture might be fulfilled, saith,*

## I thirst.

*Now there was set a vessel full of vinegar: and they filled a spunge with vinegar, and put it upon hyssop, and put it to his mouth.*

—JOHN 19:28–29

THE MOMENT WHEN JESUS SAYS "I THIRST" and is given a sponge soaked in vinegary wine on a hyssop is more complex, and more compelling, than it might first appear. In the Book of Exodus, hyssop was used to sprinkle the blood of the Passover lamb on the doorposts of the Jews to ensure God's protection.

Now there is a new Lamb of God. As Raymond E. Brown pointed out, John uses the image of hyssop—a leafy flowering plant—even though it is difficult to imagine how such a plant could "bear the weight of a soaked sponge." Here is a place in the narrative of the cross where, rather than reporting events, the evangelist is making a larger point. John opened his Gospel with John the Baptist crying, "Behold the Lamb of God!" At the end of the earthly odyssey, that Lamb is being symbolically linked to the Passover drama.

I read "I thirst" quite personally, as an emblem of the urgency and efficacy of the Holy Eucharist. When the people of God thirst, we turn to the altar and to the words of institution that Jesus used at the Last Supper, creating an act of remembrance. As Paul described it in First Corinthians,

> For I received from the Lord what I also delivered to you, that the Lord Jesus on the night when he was betrayed took bread, and when he had given thanks, he broke it, and said, "This is my body, which is for you. Do this in remembrance of me." In the same way also he took the cup, after supper, saying, "This cup is the new covenant in my blood. Do this, as often as you drink it, in remembrance of me." For as often as you eat this bread and drink the cup, you proclaim the Lord's death until he comes.

For sacramental Christians—and I am one—the Mass is the center of faith, for it is always there. Devout or distracted, ecstatic or gloomy, we are told to obey the commandment to "do this in remembrance of me," and, in so doing, we are mysteriously but unmistakably in communion with God the Father through the sacrifice of God the Son by the working of the Holy Ghost. No matter how we feel, no matter what kind of day or week we've had, our thirst is satisfied, and order is restored to a broken world, if only for a moment.

In a 1955 letter, Flannery O'Connor described attending a dinner party of New York intellectuals at Mary McCarthy's. The evening dragged on and on and ultimately the talk turned to the Eucharist. A lapsed Roman Catholic, Mary McCarthy said "when she was a child and received the Host, she thought of it as the

Holy Ghost, He being the 'most portable' person of the Trinity; now she thought of it as a symbol and implied that it was a pretty good one." An unlapsed Catholic, O'Connor related her reply to McCarthy: "I then said, in a very shaky voice, 'Well, if it's a symbol, to hell with it.' That was all the defense I was capable of but I realize now that this is all I will ever be able to say about it, outside of a story, except that it is the center of existence for me; all the rest of life is expendable."

It is unfashionable to focus too much on sin and shortcoming in mainstream theology; when the Episcopal Church reformed its Book of Common Prayer in the 1970s, it dropped a key phrase from the General Confession of Sin, one that acknowledged "there is no health in us." But John Henry Newman wrote a very different kind of prayer of humble access, and I think we learn more from the words of a dead Victorian than from the revised Confession of our own time. Before Holy Communion, Newman would pray: "Thou seest, not only the stains and scars of past sins, but the mutilations, the deep cavities, the chronic disorders which they have left in my soul. Thou seest the innumerable living sins . . . living in their power and presence, their guilt, and their penalties, which clothe me. . . . Yet Thou comest. Thou seest most perfectly. . . . Yet Thou comest."

Through the Mass, he comest everywhere, to all sorts and conditions of men. In his book *The Shape of the Liturgy,* the Anglican monk Gregory Dix wrote a prose poem to the Mass. It bears reading in its entirety. Of the command "Do this in remembrance of me," Dix observed:

Was ever another command so obeyed? For century after century, spreading slowly to every continent and country and among every race on earth, this action has been done, in every conceivable human circumstance, for every conceivable human need from infancy and before it to extreme old age and after it, from the pinnacles of earthly greatness to the refuge of fugitives in the caves and dens of the earth. Men have found no better thing than this to do for kings at their crowning and for criminals going to the scaffold; for armies in triumph or for a bride and bridegroom in a little country church; for the proclamation of a dogma or for a good crop of wheat; for the wisdom of the Parliament of a mighty nation or for a sick old woman afraid to die; for a schoolboy sitting an examination or for Columbus setting out to discover America; for the famine of whole provinces or for the soul of a dead lover; in thankfulness because my father did not die of pneumonia . . . because the Turk was at the gates of Vienna; for the repentance of Margaret; for the settlement of a strike; for a son for a barren woman; for Captain so-and-so wounded and prisoner of war; while the lions roared in the nearby amphitheater; on the beach at Dunkirk . . . tremulously, by an old monk on the fiftieth anniversary of his vows; furtively, by an exiled bishop who had hewn timber all day in a prison camp near Murmansk; gorgeously, for the canonization of St. Joan of Arc—one could fill many pages with the reasons why men have done this, and not tell a hundredth part of them. And best of all, week by week and month by month, on a hundred thousand successive Sundays, faithfully, unfailingly, across all the parishes of christendom, the pastors have done this just to make the *plebs sancta Dei*—the holy common people of God.

In a letter to a goddaughter on the occasion of her confirmation, C. S. Lewis laid out a practical understanding of the power of sacrament:

Don't expect (I mean, don't *count on* and don't *demand*) that when you are confirmed, or when you make your first Communion, you will have all the *feelings* you would like to have. You may, of course: but also you may not. But don't worry if you don't get them. They aren't what matter. The things that are happening to you are quite real things whether you feel as you wd. wish or not, just as a meal will do a hungry person good even if he has a cold in the head which will rather spoil the taste. Our Lord will give us right feelings if He wishes—and then we must say Thank you. If He doesn't, then we must say to ourselves (and Him) that He knows us best. . . . For years after I had become a regular communicant I can't tell you how dull my feelings were and how my attention wandered at the most important moments. It is only in the last year or two that things have begun to come right—which just shows how important it is to keep on doing what you are told.

Jesus thirsted and was given a bit of vinegary wine. We thirst and are given everything. He suffered that we might be saved. He died that we might live.

# THE
# SIXTH WORD

When Jesus therefore had received the vinegar, he said,

## It is finished:

and he bowed his head, and gave up the ghost.

—JOHN 19:30

WHAT, EXACTLY, WAS FINISHED, or accomplished? Those there at the hour of his death believed one thing; Christians now believe another.

So much of scripture and theology is contradictory, complex, confusing. The ways of the Almighty are inscrutable, frustrating, even maddening. It has been ever thus. In the Book of Job, the author writes:

> Can you fathom the mysteries of God? Can you probe the limits of the Almighty?
> They are higher than the heavens above—what can you do? They are deeper than the depths below—what can you know?
> Their measure is longer than the earth and wider than the sea.

Paul tells us that "the peace of God . . . surpasses all understanding." And the theologian William Porcher DuBose is said to have once been asked what he made of the Book of Revelation. "I have no idea," he reportedly replied.

But we must try. The word Jesus uses for "finished" is the perfect tense of the Greek word *tetelestai,* meaning finished, completed, or accomplished. The expected mission of the messiah was to bring about a new kingdom that would restore Israel and fulfill scriptures such as Daniel's concluding image of a day of judgment and reckoning:

> And many of them that sleep in the dust of the earth shall awake, some to everlasting life, and some to shame and everlasting contempt.
> And they that be wise shall shine as the brightness of the firmament; and they that turn many to righteousness as the stars for ever and ever.

Yet Jesus defined his own messianic work differently. In Matthew, he said, "Even as the Son of man came not to be ministered unto, but to minister, and to give his life [as] a ransom for many." And Paul, in Romans, was even more explicit, writing, "But now the righteousness of God has been manifested . . . through faith in Jesus Christ for all who believe. For there is no distinction; since all have sinned and fall short of the glory of God, they are justified by his grace as a gift, through the redemption which is in Christ Jesus, whom God put forward as an expiation by his blood, to be received by faith."

By the time of the casting of the creeds in ensuing centuries, believers would profess that Jesus was to return from heaven "to judge the quick and the dead." There is, then, more to be done. All is actually *not* finished, and this leads us to the subjects of salvation and damnation.

In earliest Christianity, the understanding of life after death was, like so much else in the young faith, the product of both Jewish and classical pagan thought and custom. According to the new vision, those who believed in Jesus were to be saved, which did not mean a glorious eternity in an ethereal region. It meant, instead, a two-step process. First, when a believer died, his body was left behind, and his soul went to a place of rest in preparation for the second phase: a bodily resurrection into "a new heaven and a new earth"—not simply into a heaven. "Heaven, in the Bible, is not a future destiny but the other, hidden dimension of our ordinary life—God's dimension, if you like," the scholar and Anglican bishop N. T. Wright has observed. "God made heaven and earth; at the last he will remake both and join them together forever." Even in the climactic images of the twenty-first and twenty-second chapters of the Book of Revelation, Wright notes, "we find not ransomed souls making their way to a disembodied heaven but rather the new Jerusalem coming down from heaven to earth, uniting the two in a lasting embrace."

This point of view is one in which the alleviation of the evident pain and injustice of the world is the ongoing work that Jesus began and that we should continue. The earth is not a temporary place that will disappear on the last day. It will, rather, merge with heaven, which means "God's space." Therefore, one should neither need nor want a ticket out of the created order into an ethereal realm. One should instead be hard at work making the world godly and just. "Of course there are people who think of 'heaven' as a kind of pie-in-the-sky dream of an afterlife to make the thought of dying less awful," Wright has written. "No doubt that's a problem as old as the human race. But in the Bible, 'heaven' isn't 'the place where people go when they die.' In the Bible heaven is God's space, while earth (or if you like, 'the cosmos' or 'creation') is our space. And the Bible makes it clear that the two overlap and inter-lock."

Which raises an interesting question: If heaven is "God's space," what about hell? Traditionally, the key to salvation is the acknowledgment that Jesus is the Son of God, who, in the words of the ancient creed, "for us and for our salvation came down from heaven . . . and was made man." In the evangelical ethos, for instance, one either accepts this and goes to heaven, or denies this and goes to hell.

From a traditionalist perspective, to take away hell is to leave the church without its most powerful sanc-tion. From the apostle Paul to John Paul II, from Au-gustine to Calvin, Christians have debated atonement and judgment for nearly two thousand years. Early in the twentieth century, Harry Emerson Fosdick, who came to represent theological liberalism, argued against biblical inerrancy and the existence of hell. It was time, progressives said, for the faith to surrender its super-natural claims. Hell was an affront to modern mores, but the liberal assertion of a looser theology produced a formidable conservative reaction, one that endures even now.

The more expansive liberal tradition holds that Jesus, the Son of God, was an atoning sacrifice for the sins of humanity, and the prospect of a place of eternal torment is irreconcilable with the God of love. Belief in Jesus should lead human beings to work for the good of this world. What comes next has to wait.

It is also true, however, that the Christian tradition since the first church has insisted that history *is* tragic for those who do not believe in Jesus; that hell is, for them, forever; and that love, in the end, will envelop those who profess Jesus as Lord, and they—and they alone—will be reconciled to God. Such views cannot be dismissed because they are inconvenient or uncomfortable.

Jesus did speak of a hell for the "condemned." "Depart from me, you cursed [ones], into the eternal fire prepared for the devil and his angels," Jesus says in Matthew. In Mark he speaks of "the unquenchable fire," and the Book of Revelation paints a vivid picture—in a visionary writing that the author says he was composing when he was "in the Spirit, on the Lord's day," a signal that, again, this is not an Associated Press report—of the lake of fire and the dismissal of the damned from the presence of God to a place where "they shall be tormented day and night for ever and ever."

And yet there is a contrary scriptural trend that

suggests, as Jesus put it, the gates of hell shall not finally prevail. (The problem with arguing from biblical texts, of course, is that the books contradict themselves. Fighting verse to verse is like a guerrilla war that never ends.) And there are references to the universal redemption of creation, a redemption that includes those who do not meet the standard requirements of confession of belief in Jesus. In Matthew, Jesus speaks of the "renewal of all things"; in Acts, Peter says God will "restore everything"; in Romans, Paul proclaims that "all Israel shall be saved"; in Colossians, the author writes that "God was pleased to . . . reconcile to himself all things, whether things on earth or things in heaven."

So which is it—heaven for Christians who say they are Christians, and hell for everybody else? What about babies, or people who died without ever hearing the gospel through no fault of their own? Who knows? We surely don't.

We must, therefore, act on the knowledge we do have, and we know that we've been told to love God totally and to love one another as ourselves—as Jesus, quoting Leviticus, teaches are the greatest commandments. On Easter, in Christian churches large and small, many hear the words of the fifteenth chapter of Paul's first letter to the Corinthians. It is about resurrection—first Jesus's, then the great resurrection that is said to await. The closing image of this mighty passage, though, is not about eternal bliss and peace but work, deeds, action: "Always give yourselves fully to the work of the Lord," Paul wrote, "because you know that your labor in the Lord is not in vain." In a vision of ultimate reward, a reminder of what is essential: performing the work that is always at hand, work that can only be truly finished when the Lord comes, whenever that might be and whatever that might mean.

# THE
# SEVENTH WORD

*And when Jesus had cried with a loud voice, he said,*

## *Father, into thy hands*
## *I commend my spirit.*

—LUKE 23:46

THE STORY, IT SEEMED, WAS OVER. With a final word entrusting his soul to the Lord, he surrendered to pain and to mortality, and died. In the same way Jesus commended his spirit to God, giving all according to the will of the Father, Christians are in many ways called to commend ourselves to the apostolic faith as it emerged from the pain and the crisis of the first decades and centuries after Jesus. Such an act of commendation is not passive; indeed, it is the most active and important thing we can possibly do, for in assenting to the truth of the Christian story we are committing ourselves to a habit of mind and of heart that tends toward love and order rather than selfishness and disorder. The philosopher William James put it well, saying, "We and God have business with each other; and in opening ourselves to his influence our deepest destiny is fulfilled."

For Jesus's followers, the shape and depth of that destiny was unclear in the wake of his final words from the cross. All was sadness and chaos. The expected kingdom, with its defeat of the world's powers and the victory of God, was not to come. Jesus, it turned out, had been talking about a different kind of kingdom, one in which the last would be first, the meek would inherit the earth, and his death would give life.

"Lo! I tell you a mystery," Paul was to write. "We shall not all sleep, but we shall all be changed, in a moment, in the twinkling of an eye, at the last trumpet."

It is surely a mystery. Jesus surrendered to the Father; we are asked to surrender to Jesus. Yes, it all requires, in Samuel Taylor Coleridge's phrase, a willing suspension of disbelief, but, when we get right down to it, what doesn't? The most secular of scientists cannot explain the mystery of creation, and yet here we are. The most religious of theologians will never fully explain the mystery of redemption, and yet here we are.

On Good Friday, with the Lord dead, there was only darkness. On the other side of the cross, though, lay light, and the enduring truth that the kingdom, which shall have no end, will come one day.

We must make our peace with mystery or else we might go mad. For me, faith is complicated, challenging, and sometimes confounding. It is not magical but mysterious. Magic means there is a spell, a formula, to work wonders. Mystery means there is no spell, no formula—only shadow and impenetrability and hope that, in a phrase T. S. Eliot borrowed from Julian of Norwich, all shall be well, and all manner of thing shall be well.

In the meantime—and that is where most of life is lived, in the meantime—whether you worship God the

Father of the Holy Trinity, the God of Abraham of Judaism, the Lord who spoke to the Prophet in the cave in the founding hours of Islam, or some other god, known only to a few, or even just to you, we all seek the means of grace, and the hope of glory.

# Even Unto the End of the World

*Why the Cross, of all deaths?*
—ATHANASIUS, FOURTH-CENTURY BISHOP
OF ALEXANDRIA

LATER, WHEN HE TRIED to get it all down on paper, Blaise Pascal wrote in bursts, capturing flashes of what he thought he had seen in the vision—a vision that, by empirical standards, could only be called fantastical. There was no doubt in Pascal's mind, though, that it had happened, and happened in time and space, in a way his mathematically trained brain conceived of things as happening. Pascal remembered the exact time—between the hours of half past ten and half past midnight on Thursday, November 23, 1654, the feast day, in the Christian calendar, of Saint Clement, pope and martyr. Jesus appeared to Pascal; God was real; the Christian story was true: "Certainty, certainty, heartfelt, joy, peace. God of Jesus Christ. God of Jesus Christ. *My God and your God.* . . . Joy, joy, joy, tears of joy." In a collection of writings found after his death, published as *Pensées,* Pascal blended his two passions, mathematics and faith, to lay out what has come to be known as Pascal's wager: It is smarter to bet that God exists, and to believe in him, because if it turns out that he is real, you win everything; if he is not, you lose nothing. So why not take the leap of faith?

Because, skeptics say, religious belief is irrational, and the faithful are living in a fairy-tale world. And other faith traditions have their own cosmologies, so who's to say what's true and what's not? Yet both atheism and differing theological worldviews are to be expected in the panoply of humanity; the decline in affiliation with traditional religious institutions in America is one of the great realities of the twenty-first century, and it is a trend I suspect will only grow.

Such a development is unsurprising; there is, as the Book of Ecclesiastes says, nothing new under the sun. The notion of *atheos* (*a*- means without; *theos* means god or gods) can be found in antiquity; Plato discusses unbelief. By the sixteenth century, as the modern era took shape, Copernicus's revelation that Earth was not the center of the universe inaugurated an age of rising skepticism about belief systems such as Christianity. By the eighteenth, Enlightenment thinkers celebrated (prematurely) the defeat of what Thomas Jefferson called "monkish ignorance and superstition." In the nineteenth, Charles Darwin published *On the Origin of Species,* and doubt was so pervasive that Matthew Arnold believed the "Sea of Faith" was in retreat, leaving only "a darkling plain . . . Where ignorant armies clash by night." The tide was barely out before Nietzsche declared God was dead.

There are many levels of argument between believers and atheists. Here are just a few. There is the holy books argument: There must be a God, the religious say, for the Bible (or the Qur'an, or any other sacred text) says so. This is the assertion of the literalist and depends on an uncritical reading of scriptures that some believers say were written (or dictated) by God. There is the moral-sense argument: There must be a God, the religious say, because human beings have an innate understanding of right and wrong, an understanding that God planted in every human heart. There is the design argument: There must be a God, the religious say, for the world is so complex and makes so much sense that there has to be a guiding intelligence at the center of it all.

I am oversimplifying, but none of these is a particularly strong proof of a deity. Scriptures are the products of human hands and hearts and have been translated and copied for generations upon generations; scholarship clearly shows us that the texts present historical and literary problems that rule out the possibility that they are perfect books. When it comes to morality, it is possible that empathy is a trait that developed in evolution as a desirable feature in forming communities that stood a better chance of thriving in the process of natural selection. On the question of design, there is no evidence, outside the Bible, to support the proposition that a creator has been in the picture, though no one knows how things got started in the very first instance. (Big bang, yes—but where did the stuff that went bang come from?)

There are religious counter-counterarguments to these counterarguments, of course; the debate goes on, world without end. With the exception of explaining the origin of the physical law and matter that brought the universe into being fourteen billion years ago, atheists can easily mock the religious for believing in fanciful stories of ascending saviors, parting seas, and burning bushes. With little trouble, atheists can pose devastating questions: If God is great, then why do babies get cancer? Why do the innocent suffer? Why do the religious kill in the name of their God, when their God is supposed to be love incarnate? Why did God stop performing miracles on a large scale once the New Testament was written?

Excellent questions all. Believers reply that God made us with free will, for love coerced is no love at all, only tyranny, and God wanted us to choose whether to love him or not, to obey him or not. Evil of human devising exists because we make reprehensible choices and have, as Paul said, fallen short of the glory of God. Evil from nature or disease is a mystery; God has not told us everything and has his own purposes beyond our understanding. If we knew everything, we would be God, not men.

These answers are fine as far as they go—but still children die, things go wrong, and hearts get broken, so the answers don't go very far. I certainly can't dispose of the challenges to Christian belief, nor can I make an entirely rational case for the existence of God. What I can do is join a vast chorus of voices who see religion as intrinsic and seek to make their home in the ethos of a faith that suggests an order and a direction amid the confusions of life.

Is God real? It seems safe to say at least this much: He is real insofar as he is a force who influences human beings who believe in his existence. In his landmark Gifford Lectures at Edinburgh in 1901–02, William James quoted a colleague on the question: "The truth of the matter can be put in this way: *God is not known, he is not understood; he is used*—sometimes as a meat-purveyor, sometimes as moral support, sometimes as friend, sometimes as an object of love. If he proves himself useful, the religious consciousness asks for no more than that. Does God really exist? How does he exist? What is he? are so many irrelevant questions. Not God, but life, more life, a larger, richer, more satisfying life, is, in the last analysis, the end of religion." And religion is not for the faint of heart; it is a hard, difficult business. It is more courageous to hope than it is to fear, more taxing to be selfless than selfish, more humbling to hold that there is more to the universe than the eye can see or the ear can hear.

And yet we have heard the last words of Jesus from the cross. That was our purpose—a devotional and admittedly discursive task in the tradition of the Christian church. Let us end with some words of unswerving faith. "Why the Cross, of all deaths?" Athanasius, a fourth-century bishop of Alexandria, asked. Because, he said, "if the Lord's death is the ransom of all, and by His death the middle wall of partition is broken down, and the calling of the nations is brought about, how would He have called us to Him, had He not been crucified? For it is only on the cross that a man dies with his hands spread out. Whence it was fitting for the Lord to bear this also and to spread out His hands, that with the one He might draw the ancient people, and with the other those from the Gentiles, and unite both in Himself." Evil was defeated, God was victorious—all by means of the cross.

So what to do now, as history unfolds? We should try to move forward with faith and with reason, knowing that we cannot answer God's taunting question of Job: "Where wast thou when I laid the foundations of the earth?" Short of the end of all things, we will never work out the contradictions evident in the story of God and of Jesus's life and Passion. God's creatures might well be, in the words of a great hymn, "ransomed, healed, restored, [and] forgiven" through the blood of Jesus, but God's creation remains a place of perplexity. Jesus, we are often taught, is the answer, but if you are anything like me you surely wish there weren't so damned many questions.

What, then, do we know for certain? That we should love one another as we would be loved, take care of the least of these, keep the feast in remembrance of Our Lord's sacrifice, and remain open, always open, to the mysterious grace of God. Yet how easy such things are to say, or to preach, and how hard, how very hard, they are to do.

No matter where one stands in terms of faith, Jesus (be he God or man or both) was perhaps the most important figure who ever drew breath. He will enthrall us to the end of time—and, if believers have it right, far beyond what William Faulkner once called "the last red and dying evening." In the Gospel of Matthew, the risen Jesus says, "Lo, I am with you always, even unto the end of the world." Is that promise, at last, an answer to Pilate's query about truth? We know this much: In the shadow of the cross, hope—not certainty, and surely not fear—is the truth that endures despite all the pain and all the heartbreak and all the tears. "In the world ye shall have tribulation," Jesus said, "but be of good cheer; I have overcome the world." Or so we pray, now and always.

# ACKNOWLEDGMENTS

These meditations were first written for delivery at St. Thomas Church Fifth Avenue on Good Friday 2013 at the invitation of the Reverend Andrew C. Mead, DD, OBE. St. Thomas was my family's beloved parish in New York City for fifteen years. Andrew is a friend from whom I have learned much, and I am thankful for his guidance and grace. My wife and I are also indebted to the Reverend Robert H. Stafford, to Richard Somerset-Ward, and to the late Reverend Canon John G. B. Andrew for their steadfast friendship at St. Thomas.

I am also grateful for invitations to speak from sundry pulpits through the years, experiences that enabled me to work through the themes that inform this book: St. John's Church, Lafayette Square, Washington, D.C.; Trinity Church Wall Street; All Saints' Chapel, Sewanee, Tennessee; St. Paul's Episcopal Church, Chattanooga; St. Martin's Episcopal Church, Houston; Washington National Cathedral; Nashotah House Theological Seminary, Nashotah, Wisconsin; St. Ann's Episcopal Church, Kennebunkport; and St. George's Episcopal Church, Nashville, my family's parish; and for the opportunities I have had to address meetings of the

Anti-Defamation League in New York, Washington, and elsewhere around the country. I thank Luis Leon, James Cooper, Joel Cunningham, Tom Macfie, Hunter Huckabay, Russell Levenson, Randolph Hollerith, Peter Cheney, Leigh Spruill, and ADL president Abraham Foxman for their hospitality on these occasions.

For this project I also drew on several of my previous writings for *The New York Times Book Review, Newsweek, Time,* and *The Washington Post.* I am grateful to my editors and colleagues at each publication for their generosity, assistance, and willingness to devote valuable space and resources to these matters.

I have long been the beneficiary of the scholarship and friendly counsel of Paula Fredriksen, the Aurelio Professor of Scripture emerita at Boston University, and of N. T. Wright, Research Professor of New Testament and Early Christianity at St. Mary's College in the University of St. Andrews in Scotland, and sometime Anglican bishop of Durham, England. Both have been generous in the past and both kindly advised me on these meditations. They of course bear no responsibility for anything I have written, but I am indebted to them for their remarkable work and for their personal grace.

As I have noted elsewhere, I owe much of my initial interest in theology and history to the late Professor the Reverend Doctor Herbert S. Wentz of The University of the South. Herbert's insistence on clarity, precision, and intellectual honesty in writing about religion—and everything else—has long given me a standard to which to aspire. I'm sure I've fallen short many times and will again. But if I do manage to hit the mark, I do so in large measure because of Herbert and because of a company of remarkable teachers: Dale Richardson, John Reishman, Pamela Macfie, Robert Benson, Charles Perry, Samuel Williamson, and the late Eric Naylor, Douglas Paschall, Joseph Cushman, Charles Binnicker, and Willie Cocke. I am also mindful of my debts to the Most Reverend John M. Allin, VI Bishop of Mississippi and XXIII Presiding Bishop of the Episcopal Church, and to John Strang, who taught me the Bible in the seventh grade at the McCallie School. Known affectionately as "Yo," Mr. Strang had a favorite extra-credit question: Who was on the road to Damascus, and where was Saul going? It pains me to say not all of us got it the first time around, but Yo kept asking, thus embodying, as was his wont, the gospel promise of redemption and restoration.

My thanks to Jay Wellons and Brock Kidd, friends who were early readers of these pages. Merrill Fabry brilliantly fact-checked the manuscript. At Random House, my publisher for two decades, I am grateful to Gina Centrello, Kate Medina, Bill Takes, Porscha Burke, Tina Constable, Campbell Wharton, Keren Baltzer, Dennis Ambrose, Carole Lowenstein, Carol Poticny, Cynthia Lasky, Todd Berman, Lori Addicott, Rebecca Berlant, Jessica Bright, Daniel Christensen, Andrea DeWerd, Benjamin Dreyer, Michael Harney, Cindy Murray, Joe Perez, Minhee Bae, Paolo Pepe, Sandra Sjursen, and Stacey Witcraft.

# NOTES

## EPIGRAPH

ix     "FOR NOW WE SEE" I Corinthians 13:12, KJV.

ix     IT IS FAR BETTER Robert Louis Wilken, *The Spirit of Early Christian Thought: Seeking the Face of God* (New Haven, Conn., 2003), 14.


## PROLOGUE

3     "BUT WE PREACH CHRIST CRUCIFIED" I Corinthians 1:23–27, KJV.

3     "IN THE WORLD" John 16:33, KJV.

5     "SO YOU ARE A KING?" John 18:37, RSV. My understanding of the Passion owes much to Paula Fredriksen, *Jesus of Nazareth, King of the Jews: A Jewish Life and the Emergence of Christianity* (New York, 1999), and *When Christians Were Jews: The First Generation* (New Haven, Conn., 2018).

5     "WHAT IS TRUTH?" John 18:38, RSV.

5     "ALL MEN NEED THE GODS" Homer, *The Odyssey*, trans. Robert Fagles (New York, 1996), 109.

6     "GODS," THE PROTESTANT THEOLOGIAN PAUL TILLICH Paul Tillich, *Systematic Theology*, vol. 1, *Reason and Revelation, Being and God* (Chicago, 1973), 212.

6     THIS BOOK IS A SERIES OF REFLECTIONS I am indebted to a number of works for the arguments I am putting forward. See, in particular, Saint Robert Bellarmine, *The Seven Last Words from the Cross* (Providence, R.I., 2016); Raymond E. Brown, *A Cruci-fied Christ in Holy Week: Essays on the Four Gospel Passion Narratives* (Collegeville, Minn., 1986); Brown, *The Death of the Messiah: From Gethsemane to the Grave; A Commentary on the Passion Narratives in the Four Gospels*, 2 vols. (New York, 1994); Brown, *An Introduction to*

*the Gospel of John,* ed. Francis J. Moloney (New York, 2003); Brown, *An Introduction to the New Testament* (New York, 1997); Christopher Bryan, *The Resurrection of the Messiah* (New York, 2011); Craig A. Evans and N. T. Wright, *Jesus, the Final Days: What Really Happened,* ed. Troy A. Miller (Louisville, Ky., 2009); Fredriksen, *Jesus of Nazareth* and *When Christians Were Jews;* Richard John Neuhaus, *Death on a Friday Afternoon: Meditations on the Last Words of Jesus from the Cross* (New York, 2000); Robert Louis Wilken, *The Christians as the Romans Saw Them* (New Haven, Conn., 1984); Wilken, *Spirit of Early Christian Thought;* N. T. Wright, *The Day the Revolution Began: Reconsidering the Meaning of Jesus's Crucifixion* (San Francisco, 2016); Wright, *Simply Christian: Why Christianity Makes Sense* (New York, 2006); Wright, *Christian Origins and the Question of God,* vol. 3, *The Resurrection of the Son of God* (Minneapolis, 2003); among others.

7    "IT DOES ME NO INJURY" Thomas Jefferson, *Notes on the State of Virginia,* ed. William Peden (Chapel Hill, 1955), 159.

7    "EXPERIENCE TEACHES US" Amanda Porterfield, *Conceived in Doubt: Religion and Politics in the New American Nation* (Chicago, 2012), 152.

7    "WE CANNOT ATTAIN" Wilken, *Christians as the Romans Saw Them,* 163.

8    "I KNOW THAT" Job 19:25, KJV.

8    "THE CHRIST, THE SON OF THE LIVING GOD" Matthew 16:16, KJV.

9    "A NEW HEAVEN AND A NEW EARTH" Revelation 21:1, KJV.

9    "JESUS MEANS SOMETHING" Albert Schweitzer, *The Quest of the Historical Jesus,* trans. W. Montgomery (1910; repr., Mineola, N.Y., 2005), 397.

9    "THE STRANGE FACT" A. N. Wilson, *Jesus: A Life* (New York, 1992), 4.

9    JESUS'S MISSION, AS DEFINED BY PAUL See, for instance, Wright, *Day the Revolution Began,* 73–142.

9    "AND I WILL MAKE" Genesis 12:2–3, KJV.

10   "FOR I DELIVERED TO YOU" 1 Corinthians 15:3–5, RSV.

10   "FOR GOD SO LOVED" John 3:16, KJV.

11   "THE SHIELD OF FAITH" Ephesians 6:16, RSV.

11   "DID NOT MAKE IT EASY" Abraham Joshua Heschel, *Moral Grandeur and Spiritual Audacity: Essays,* ed. Susannah Heschel (New York, 1996), 300.

11   "MAY WE KNOW" Acts 17:19–32, NRSV.

12    "THERE ARE MORE THINGS" William Shakespeare, *The Tragedy of Hamlet, Prince of Denmark,* http://shakespeare.mit.edu/hamlet/full.html.

12    "REASON'S LAST STEP" Blaise Pascal, *Pensées,* trans. A. J. Krailsheimer (New York, 1995), 56.

13    "OUR KNOWLEDGE IS IMPERFECT" 1 Corinthians 13:9, RSV.

13    "PRINCIPALITIES AND POWERS" Ephesians 3:10, KJV.

14    CONVICTED OF SEDITION For the points in this section, I am particularly indebted to Paula Fredriksen and N. T. Wright—both to their books and for their generous counsel to me over the years.

15    "THE WILDERNESS AND THE DRY LAND" Isaiah 35:1–10, ESV.

16    "HOW BEAUTIFUL UPON" Isaiah 52:7–10, ESV.

16    "O SING UNTO" Psalm 98:1–9, KJV.

18    "THIS NEWS WOULD" Fredriksen, *Jesus of Nazareth, King of the Jews,* 251–52.

18    "ON THESE FESTIVE OCCASIONS" Ibid., 252.

18    "JESUS TEACHES IN" Ibid., 252–53.

19    "THE PILGRIM THRONG" Ibid., 259.

19    "FOR THE LORD HIMSELF" First Thessalonians 4:16-17, KJV.

20    "DO NOT BE AMAZED" Mark 16:6, RSV.

20    "WENT OUT AND FLED" Mark 16:8, RSV.

20    "AN IDLE TALE" Luke 24:11, ESV.

20    "AS YET . . . DID NOT KNOW" John 20:9, RSV.

21    THE NICENE CREED The quotation here is from the creed as it appeared in the Book of Common Prayer, 1662.

21    SOME DISCIPLES STILL "DOUBTED" Matthew 28:17, NRSV.

22    "THE SON OF MAN IS DELIVERED" Mark 9:31, KJV.

22    "UNDERSTOOD NOT THAT SAYING" Mark 9:32, KJV.

22    "BUT WE PREACH CHRIST CRUCIFIED" 1 Corinthians 1:23, KJV.

22    "GAVE HIMSELF FOR OUR SINS" Galatians 1:4, ESV.

23    "AND GOD SHALL WIPE AWAY" Revelation 21:4–5, KJV.

24    "HE WAS WOUNDED" Isaiah 53:5, KJV. In the Book of Acts, Peter is able to preach a sermon in which Jesus is connected to passages from Isaiah, Joel, and the Psalms. See Acts 2:14–41.

24    "I SAW IN THE NIGHT" Daniel 7:13–14, ESV.

25    "THE CHURCH REPROVES" Paul VI, *Nostra Aetate,* October 28, 1965, http://www.vatican.va/archive/hist_councils/ii_vatican_council/documents/vat-ii_decl_19651028_nostra-aetate_en.html.

25    "AS REGARDS ELECTION" Romans 11:28–29, ESV.

25    "NEITHER JEW NOR GREEK" Galatians 3:28, ESV.

25    "WERE COVERED IN" Brian Moynahan, *The Faith: A History of Christianity* (New York, 2002), 73.

26    "THE SON OF MAN MUST SUFFER" Luke 9:22, KJV.

26    "I AM THE LIVING BREAD" John 6:51, KJV.

26    "HOW UNSEARCHABLE" Romans 11:33, ESV.

26    "SEEK THE LORD" Psalm 105:4, KJV.

26    "BE AT PEACE" 1 Thessalonians, 5:13–22, RSV.

27    SIX TO EIGHT FEET HIGH William D. Edwards, MD, Wesley J. Gabel, MDiv, Floyd E. Hosmer, MS, AMI, "On the Physical Death of Jesus Christ," *Journal of the American Medical Association* 255, no. 11 (March 21, 1986): 1458.

28    "IT IS NOT THAT" Schweitzer, *Quest of the Historical Jesus,* 6.

28–29 "THESE ARE WRITTEN" John 20:31, RSV.

29    DATES AT LEAST FROM THE MIDDLE AGES Bellarmine, *Seven Last Words from the Cross,* xxvii.

29    "THE LAST SERMON" Ibid., xxv.

30    THE LAST WORDS HAVE INSPIRED Neuhaus, *Death on a Friday Afternoon,* xiii.

30    "LIFTED UP HIS EYES TO HEAVEN" John 17:1, KJV.


## THE FIRST WORD

33    "AND THERE WERE ALSO TWO OTHER" Luke 23:32–38, NKJV.

35    JESUS'S FIRST REMARK See, for instance, Brown, *Death of the Messiah,* 2:971–81.

35    "REPENT," HE SAID Matthew 4:17, KJV.

35    "AND WHEN YE SHALL HEAR" Mark 13:7–30, KJV.

36    WAKE OF ANTI-ROMAN ACTIVITY See, for instance, Mark 15:7.

36    IF JESUS HAD TRULY BEEN I am indebted to Fredriksen for much of this analysis. See, for instance, *When Christians Were Jews,* 57–73.

37    "THE SCRIBE OF" Brown, *Introduction to the New Testament,* 267.

37    "LOVE YOUR ENEMIES" Brown, *Death of the Messiah,* 2:976; Luke 6:27–29, NIV.

38    LUKE WRITES OF SAINT STEPHEN'S SIMILAR PRAYER Acts 7:60, KJV. See also Brown, *Death of the Messiah,* 2:976.

38    "LORD, GOD, FATHER, FORGIVE THEM" Brown, *Death of the Messiah,* 2:977.

40    "MY SOUL DOTH MAGNIFY" Luke 1:46–47, KJV.

40    "BLESSED BE THE LORD GOD OF ISRAEL" Luke 1:68–71, KJV.

40     "AND THERE WERE IN THE SAME COUNTRY" Luke 2:8–14, KJV.

42     "HEAVEN AND EARTH SHALL PASS AWAY" Luke 21:33, KJV.

43     "ALL SCRIPTURE IS" 2 Timothy 3:16–17, NIV.

43     "WHOEVER THINKS HE" Eleonore Stump and Norman Kretzmann, eds., *The Cambridge Companion to Augustine* (Cambridge, 2001), 67–68.

44     "TO SEARCH OUT" Paul VI, *Dei Verbum,* November 18, 1965, http://www.vatican.va/archive/hist_councils/ii_vatican_council/documents/vat-ii_const_19651118_dei-verbum_en.html.

44     HEARD, READ, MARKED From the Collect for the Second Sunday of Advent, Book of Common Prayer, 1549.

## THE SECOND WORD

47     "THEN ONE OF THE CRIMINALS" Luke 23:39–43, NKJV.

49     CRUCIFIXION WAS BRUTAL See, for instance, Martin Hengel, *Crucifixion in the Ancient World and the Folly of the Message of the Cross* (Philadelphia, 1977), and Edwards, Gabel, and Hosmer, "On the Physical Death of Jesus Christ," 1455–63.

49     TO ROME, . . . THE *CRUX* Hengel, *Crucifixion,* 33.

49     "CAN ANY MAN BE FOUND" Ibid., 31.

49     "THE USUAL INSTRUMENT" Edwards, Gabel, and Hosmer, "On the Physical Death of Jesus Christ," 1457.

50     THE CONDEMNED WAS TYPICALLY Ibid., 1458–59.

50     THE CRUCIFIED TENDED TO DIE Ibid., 1461.

50     CICERO REFERRED TO Hengel, *Crucifixion,* 36–37.

50     "SATISFIED THE PRIMITIVE LUST" Ibid., 87.

50     ONE OF THE MEN CALLS OUT Brown, *Death of the Messiah,* 2:999–1013.

51     THERE HAD BEEN A RECENT REBELLION See, for instance, Mark 15:7.

52     AND THE TERM "PARADISE" Ibid., 1010.

52     "HE THAT HATH AN EAR" Revelation 2:7, KJV.

## THE THIRD WORD

55     "NOW THERE STOOD" John 19: 25–27, KJV.

57     "YOU THINK OF YOURSELF" John Henry Newman, *Meditations and Devotions* (Springfield, Ill., 1964), x–xi.

58     DOERS OF THE WORD James 1:22, KJV.

58    "Then the King will say" Matthew 25:34–43, RSV.

59    "Come and see" John 1:39, KJV.

59    "Finally, brethren, whatever" Philippians 4:8, RSV.

59    "I believe in one God" Walter Isaacson, ed., *A Benjamin Franklin Reader* (New York, 2003), 376–78.

## THE FOURTH WORD

63    "Now from the sixth hour" Matthew 27:45–46, KJV.

65    "cry" or "shout" is usually used Brown, *Death of the Messiah,* 2:1044–45.

65    When Jesus raised Lazarus Ibid., 1045.

65    "cried with a loud voice" John 11:43, KJV.

65    in First Thessalonians Brown, *Death of the Messiah,* 2:1045.

65    "the Lord himself" First Thessalonians, 4:16, KJV.

65    "O clap your hands" Psalm 47:1–3, KJV.

66    What we can say Brown, *Death of the Messiah,* 2:1048–51.

66    "is whether the struggle" Ibid., 1049.

67    The Greek meaning of the term Edward Robinson, *A Greek and English Lexicon of the New Testament* (New York, 1870), 30.

67    "Deliver my soul" Psalm 22:20–28, KJV.

## THE FIFTH WORD

73    "After this, Jesus" John 19:28–29, KJV.

75    hyssop was used to Brown, *Death of the Messiah,* 2:1074–77.

75    "bear the weight" Ibid., 1075.

75    "Behold the Lamb of God!" John 1:36, KJV.

76    "For I received" 1 Corinthians 11:23–26, RSV.

76    In a 1955 letter Flannery O'Connor, *The Habit of Being: Letters,* ed. Sally Fitzgerald (New York, 1979), 125.

77    "Thou seest, not only" Newman, *Meditations and Devotions,* vi.

78    "Was ever another command" Gregory Dix, *The Shape of the Liturgy* (Westminster [London], 1945), 744–45.

79    "Don't expect" C. S. Lewis, *C. S. Lewis Letters to Children* (New York, 1995), 26.

## THE SIXTH WORD

83    "When Jesus therefore" John 19:30, KJV.

85    "Can you fathom" Job 11:7–9, NIV.

85    "the peace of God" Philippians 4:7, ESV.

85    THE GREEK WORD *TETELESTAI* *Strong's Concordance,* https://bible hub.com/greek/5055.htm.

86    "AND MANY OF THEM" Daniel 12:2–3, KJV.

86    "EVEN AS THE SON OF MAN" Matthew 20:28, KJV.

86    "BUT NOW THE RIGHTEOUSNESS" Romans 3:21–26, RSV.

87    "HEAVEN, IN THE BIBLE" N. T. Wright, *Surprised by Hope: Rethinking Heaven, the Resurrection, and the Mission of the Church* (New York, 2014), 19.

87    "WE FIND NOT" Ibid.

88    "OF COURSE THERE ARE PEOPLE" "N. T. Wright's Response to Stephen Hawking on Heaven," May 2011, https://www.the gospelcoalition.org/blogs/justin-taylor/n-t-wrights-response -to-stephen-hawking-on-heaven/.

89    JESUS DID SPEAK See, for instance, Alan E. Bernstein, *The Formation of Hell: Death and Retribution in the Ancient and Early Christian Worlds* (Ithaca, N.Y., 1993), and Rob Bell, *Love Wins: A Book About Heaven, Hell, and the Fate of Every Person Who Ever Lived* (New York, 2011).

89    "DEPART FROM ME" Matthew 25:41, RSV.

89    "THE UNQUENCHABLE FIRE" Mark 9:43, ESV.

89    "IN THE SPIRIT" Revelation 1:10, ESV.

89    THE LAKE OF FIRE Revelation 20:10, KJV.

89    "THEY SHALL BE TORMENTED" Ibid.

90    THE GATES OF HELL Matthew 16:18, KJV.

90    "RENEWAL OF ALL THINGS" Matthew 19:28, NIV.

90    "RESTORE EVERYTHING" Acts 3:21, NIV.

90    "ALL ISRAEL SHALL BE SAVED" Romans 11:26, KJV.

90    "GOD WAS PLEASED" Colossians 1:19–20, NIV.

90    "ALWAYS GIVE YOURSELVES" 1 Corinthians 15:58, NIV.

## THE SEVENTH WORD

93    "AND WHEN JESUS" Luke 23:46, KJV.

95    "WE AND GOD HAVE BUSINESS" William James, *The Varieties of Religious Experience: A Study in Human Nature* (New York, 1905), 516–17.

96    "LO! I TELL YOU A MYSTERY" 1 Corinthians 15:51–52, RSV.

96    A WILLING SUSPENSION OF DISBELIEF Samuel Taylor Coleridge, *Biographia Literaria; or, Biographical Sketches of My Literary Life and Opinions* (London, 1817), 2:6.

96    ALL SHALL BE WELL T. S. Eliot, "Four Quartets," *T. S. Eliot: Collected Poems, 1909–1962* (New York, 1963), 209.

## EPILOGUE

99    "WHY THE CROSS, OF ALL DEATHS?" *St. Athanasius on the Incarnation,* trans. Archibald Robertson (London, 1891), 42–43.

101    LATER, WHEN HE TRIED Pascal, *Pensées,* 285–86.

102    PLATO DISCUSSES UNBELIEF Tim Whitmarsh, *Battling the Gods: Atheism in the Ancient World* (New York, 2015), 4.

102    "MONKISH IGNORANCE AND SUPERSTITION" Thomas Jefferson to Roger C. Weightman, June 24, 1826, https://www.loc.gov/exhibits/declara/rcwltr.html.

102    THE "SEA OF FAITH" Matthew Arnold, "Dover Beach," https://www.poetryfoundation.org/poems/43588/dover-beach.

105    "THE TRUTH OF THE MATTER" James, *Varieties of Religious Experience,* 506–7.

105    "WHY THE CROSS, OF ALL DEATHS?" *St. Athanasius on the Incarnation,* 42–43.

106    "WHERE WAST THOU" Job 38:4, KJV.

106    "RANSOMED, HEALED, RESTORED" Henry Francis Lyte, "Praise, My Soul, the King of Heaven," https://hymnary.org/text/praise_my_soul_the_king_of_heaven.

107    "THE LAST RED" William Faulkner, Nobel Prize Banquet Address, December 10, 1950. https://www.nobelprize.org/prizes/literature/1949/faulkner/speech/.

107    "LO, I AM WITH YOU" Matthew 28:20, KJV.

107    "IN THE WORLD" John 16:33, KJV.

# BIBLIOGRAPHY

## BOOKS

Athanasius. *St. Athanasius on the Incarnation.* Translated by Archibald Robertson. London: David Nutt, 1891.

Attridge, Harold W., et al. *HarperCollins Study Bible: Fully Revised and Updated.* New York: HarperOne, 2017.

Augustine. *Confessions.* Translated by Henry Chadwick. Oxford World's Classics. Oxford: Oxford University Press, 1998.

Bell, Rob. *Love Wins: A Book About Heaven, Hell, and the Fate of Every Person Who Ever Lived.* New York: HarperOne, 2011.

Bellarmine, Robert. *The Seven Last Words from the Cross.* Providence, R.I.: Cluny Media, 2016.

Bernard of Clairvaux, Saint. *Five Books on Consideration: Advice to a Pope.* Translated by John D. Anderson and Elizabeth Kennan. The Works of Bernard of Clairvaux, vol. 13. Kalamazoo, Mich.: Cistercian Publications, 1976.

Bernstein, Alan E. *The Formation of Hell: Death and Retribution in the Ancient and Early Christian Worlds.* Ithaca, N.Y.: Cornell University Press, 1993.

Brown, Raymond E. *A Crucified Christ in Holy Week: Essays on the Four Gospel Passion Narratives.* Collegeville, Minn.: Liturgical Press, 1986.

———. *The Death of the Messiah: From Gethsemane to the Grave; A Commentary on the Passion Narratives in the Four Gospels.* 2 vols. Anchor Bible Reference Library. New York: Doubleday, 1994.

———. *An Introduction to the Gospel of John.* Edited and updated by Francis J. Moloney. New York: Doubleday, 2003.

———. *An Introduction to the New Testament.* The Anchor Bible Reference Library. New York: Doubleday, 1997.

Bryan, Christopher. *The Resurrection of the Messiah.* New York: Oxford University Press, 2011.

Coleridge, Samuel Taylor. *Biographia Literaria; or Biographical Sketches of My Literary Life and Opinions.* Vol. 2. London: Rest Fenner, 1817.

Dix, Gregory. *The Shape of the Liturgy.* Westminster [London]: Dacre Press, 1945.

Eliot, T. S. *Collected Poems, 1909–1962.* New York: Harcourt, Brace & World, 1963.

Evans, Craig A., and N. T. Wright. *Jesus, the Final Days: What Really Happened.* Edited by Troy A. Miller. Louisville, Ky.: Westminster John Knox Press, 2009.

Franklin, Benjamin. *A Benjamin Franklin Reader.* Edited by Walter Isaacson. New York: Simon & Schuster, 2003.

Fredriksen, Paula. *Jesus of Nazareth, King of the Jews: A Jewish Life and the Emergence of Christianity.* New York: Alfred A. Knopf, 1999.

———, ed. *On* The Passion of the Christ: *Exploring the Issues Raised by the Controversial Movie.* Berkeley: University of California Press, 2006.

———. *When Christians Were Jews: The First Generation.* New Haven, Conn.: Yale University Press, 2018.

Hengel, Martin. *Crucifixion in the Ancient World and the Folly of the Message of the Cross.* Philadelphia: Fortress Press, 1977.

Heschel, Abraham Joshua. *Moral Grandeur and Spiritual Audacity: Essays.* Edited by Susannah Heschel. New York: Farrar, Straus & Giroux, 1996.

Homer. *The Odyssey.* Translated by Robert Fagles. New York: Viking, 1996.

Hurtado, Larry W. *Lord Jesus Christ: Devotion to Jesus in Earliest Christianity.* Grand Rapids, Mich.: W. B. Eerdmans, 2003.

James, William. *The Varieties of Religious Experience: A Study in Human Nature; Being the Gifford Lectures on Natural Religion Delivered at Edinburgh in 1901–1902.* New York: Longmans, Green, 1905.

Jefferson, Thomas. *Notes on the State of Virginia.* 1787. Reprint, edited by William Peden. Chapel Hill: University of North Carolina Press, 1955.

Johnson, Paul. *A History of Christianity.* New York: Atheneum, 1976.

Kelly, Henry Ansgar. *Satan: A Biography.* Cambridge: Cambridge University Press, 2006.

Levine, Amy-Jill, and Marc Zvi Brettler, eds. *The Jewish Annotated New Testament: New Revised Standard Version Bible Translation.* 2nd ed. Oxford: Oxford University Press, 2017.

Lewis, C. S. *C. S. Lewis Letters to Children.* Edited by Lyle W. Dorsett and Marjorie Lamp Mead. New York: Simon & Schuster, 1995.

MacCulloch, Diarmaid. *Christianity: The First Three Thousand Years.* New York: Penguin, 2011.

Martin, James. *Seven Last Words: An Invitation to a Deeper Friendship with Jesus.* New York: HarperOne, 2016.

McDannell, Colleen, and Bernhard Lang. *Heaven: A History.* 2nd ed. New Haven, Conn.: Yale University Press, 2001.

McKenzie, Steven L. *How to Read the Bible: History, Prophecy, Literature— Why Modern Readers Need to Know the Difference, and What It Means for Faith Today.* Oxford: Oxford University Press, 2005.

Meier, John P. *A Marginal Jew: Rethinking the Historical Jesus.* 5 vols. The Anchor Bible Reference Library. New York: Doubleday, 1991– 2016.

Moynahan, Brian. *The Faith: A History of Christianity.* New York: Doubleday, 2002.

Neuhaus, Richard John. *Death on a Friday Afternoon: Meditations on the Last Words of Jesus from the Cross.* New York: Basic Books, 2000.

Newman, John Henry. *Meditations and Devotions.* Springfield, Ill.: Templegate, 1964.

O'Connor, Flannery. *The Habit of Being: Letters.* Edited by Sally Fitzgerald. New York: Farrar, Straus & Giroux, 1979.

Pagels, Elaine H. *The Gnostic Gospels.* 1979. Reprint, New York: Vintage Books, 1989.

Pascal, Blaise. *Pensées.* Rev. ed. Translated by A. J. Krailsheimer. Penguin Classics. New York: Penguin Books, 1995.

Pelikan, Jaroslav. *The Christian Tradition: A History of the Development of Doctrine.* Vol. 1, *The Emergence of the Catholic Tradition (100–600).* Chicago: University of Chicago Press, 1971.

———. *Whose Bible Is It?: A Short History of the Scriptures.* New York: Penguin Books, 2006.

Porterfield, Amanda. *Conceived in Doubt: Religion and Politics in the New American Nation.* American Beginnings, 1500–1900. Chicago: University of Chicago Press, 2012.

Robinson, Edward. *A Greek and English Lexicon of the New Testament.* Rev. ed. New York: Harper & Brothers, 1870.

Robinson, John A. T. *Redating the New Testament.* Philadelphia: Westminster Press, 1976.

Safire, William. *The First Dissident: The Book of Job in Today's Politics.* New York: Random House, 1992.

Sanders, E. P. *The Historical Figure of Jesus.* New York: Penguin Books, 1996.

Schweitzer, Albert. *The Quest of the Historical Jesus.* Translated by W. Montgomery. 1910. Reprint, Mineola, N.Y.: Dover, 2005.

Smith, Huston. *The World's Religions: Our Great Wisdom Traditions.* Rev. and updated ed. of *The Religions of Man,* 1958. San Francisco: HarperSanFrancisco, 1991.

Stark, Rodney. *The Rise of Christianity: How the Obscure, Marginal Jesus Movement Became the Dominant Religious Force in the Western World in a Few Centuries.* San Francisco: HarperCollins, 1996.

———. *The Victory of Reason: How Christianity Led to Freedom, Capitalism, and Western Success.* New York: Random House, 2006.

Strong, James. *The New Strong's Exhaustive Concordance of the Bible.* Nashville: Thomas Nelson, 1990.

Stump, Eleonore, and Norman Kretzmann, eds. *The Cambridge Companion to Augustine.* Cambridge Companions Series. Cambridge: Cambridge University Press, 2001.

Tillich, Paul. *Systematic Theology.* 3 vols. Chicago: University of Chicago Press, 1951–63.

Vermès, Géza. *Jesus the Jew: A Historian's Reading of the Gospels.* 1973. Reprint, Philadelphia: Fortress Press, 1981.

———. *The Real Jesus: Then and Now.* Minneapolis: Fortress Press, 2010.

Weigel, George. *The Courage to Be Catholic: Crisis, Reform, and the Future of the Church.* New York: Basic Books, 2004.

———. *Evangelical Catholicism: Deep Reform in the 21st-Century Church.* New York: Basic Books, 2013.

Whitmarsh, Tim. *Battling the Gods: Atheism in the Ancient World.* New York: Vintage Books, 2016.

Wilken, Robert Louis. *The Christians as the Romans Saw Them.* New Haven, Conn.: Yale University Press, 1984.

———. *The Spirit of Early Christian Thought: Seeking the Face of God.* New Haven, Conn.: Yale University Press, 2003.

Willis, John Randolph, SJ, ed. *The Teachings of the Church Fathers.* New York: Herder and Herder, 1966.

Wilson, A. N. *Jesus: A Life.* New York: W.W. Norton, 1992.

Wright, N. T., *Christian Origins and the Question of God.* 4 vols. Minneapolis: Fortress Press, 1992–2013.

———. *The Day the Revolution Began: Reconsidering the Meaning of Jesus's Crucifixion.* San Francisco: HarperOne, 2016.

———. *Evil and the Justice of God.* Downers Grove, Ill.: IVP Books, 2006.

———. *How God Became King: The Forgotten Story of the Gospels.* New York: HarperOne, 2012.

———. *Justification: God's Plan and Paul's Vision.* Downer's Grove, Ill.: IVP Academic, 2009.

———. *The Last Word: Beyond the Bible Wars to a New Understanding of the Authority of Scripture.* San Francisco: HarperSanFrancisco, 2005.

———. *Simply Christian: Why Christianity Makes Sense.* New York: Harper-One, 2006.

———. *Surprised by Hope: Rethinking Heaven, the Resurrection, and the Mission of the Church.* New York: HarperOne, 2008.

Wroe, Ann. *Pilate: The Biography of an Invented Man.* London: Vintage, 2000.


## ARTICLE

Edwards, William D., Wesley J. Gabel, and Floyd E. Hosmer. "On the Physical Death of Jesus Christ." *Journal of the American Medical Association* 255, no. 11 (March 21, 1986): 1455–63.


## WEBSITES

Arnold, Matthew. "Dover Beach." Poetry Foundation. https://www.poetryfoundation.org/poems/43588/dover-beach.

Jefferson, Thomas. "Declaring Independence: Drafting the Documents" [Letter from Thomas Jefferson to Roger C. Weightman, June 24, 1826]. Library of Congress. http://www.loc.gov/exhibits/declara/rcwltr.html.

Lyte, Henry Francis. "Praise, My Soul, the King of Heaven." Hymnary.org. https://hymnary.org/text/praise_my_soul_the_king_of_heaven.

Paul VI. *Dei Verbum.* The Holy See. November 18, 1965. http://www.vatican.va/archive/hist_councils/ii_vatican_council/documents/vat-ii_const_19651118_dei-verbum_en.html.

———. *Nostra Aetate.* The Holy See. October 28, 1965. http://www.vatican.va/archive/hist_councils/ii_vatican_council/documents/vat-ii_decl_19651028_nostra-aetate_en.html.

Shakespeare, William. *The Tragedy of Hamlet, Prince of Denmark.* The Complete Works of William Shakespeare. http://shakespeare.mit.edu/hamlet/full.html.

Taylor, Justin. "N. T. Wright's Response to Stephen Hawking on Heaven." *The Gospel Coalition* (blog), May 19, 2011. https://www.thegospelcoalition.org/blogs/justin-taylor/n-t-wrights-response-to-stephen-hawking-on-heaven/.

# ILLUSTRATION CREDITS

# ABOUT THE AUTHOR

JON MEACHAM is a Pulitzer Prize–winning biographer. The author of the *New York Times* bestsellers *American Gospel: God, the Founding Fathers, and the Making of a Nation; Thomas Jefferson: The Art of Power; American Lion: Andrew Jackson in the White House; Franklin and Winston: An Intimate Portrait of an Epic Friendship; Destiny and Power: The American Odyssey of George Herbert Walker Bush;* and *The Soul of America: The Battle for Our Better Angels,* Meacham holds the Carolyn T. and Robert M. Rogers Chair in the American Presidency and is a distinguished visiting professor at Vanderbilt University. Educated at The University of the South, he is a former member of the vestries of St. Thomas Church Fifth Avenue and of Trinity Church Wall Street and was honored by the Anti-Defamation League with its Hubert H. Humphrey First Amendment Freedoms Prize. A contributing writer to *The New York Times Book Review,* a contributing editor to *Time,* and a fellow of the Society of American Historians, Meacham lives in Nashville with his wife and children.

## ABOUT THE TYPE

This book was set in Requiem, a typeface designed by the Hoefler Type Foundry. It is a modern typeface inspired by inscriptional capitals in Ludovico Vicentino degli Arrighi's 1523 writing manual, *Il modo de temperare le penne*. An original lowercase, a set of figures, and an italic in the chancery style that Arrighi (fl. 1522) helped popularize were created to make this adaptation of a classical design into a complete font family.